6 SECRETS OF PRETEEN MINISTRY

SARAH FLANNERY

6 Secrets of Preteen Ministry

Editor: L. J. Zimmerman
Designers: Kellie Green and Kent Sneed

All Web addresses were correct and operational at the time of publication.

Paperback: ISBN 9781501845963
ePub: ISBN 9781501845970

17 18 19 20 21 22 23 24 25 26—10 9 8 7 6 5 4 3 2 1

MANUFACTURED IN THE UNITED STATES OF AMERICA

CONTENTS

CHAPTER 1

ADAPT

> When I was a child, I used to speak like a child,
> reason like a child, think like a child. But now that
> I have become a man, I've put an end to childish
> things. *(1 Corinthians 13:11)*

It's spectacular that in the most famous passage on love in the Bible, Paul digresses for just a moment to give us a spot-on description of what it's like to be a preteen. In this stage, kids aren't just growing— they're growing up. And that means saying goodbye to the activities, toys, ideas, and sometimes friends that they depended on when they were younger. It means changing their focus from the present to the future, sometimes with anxiety and sometimes with excitement. It means putting an end to childish things.

Doesn't this very next verse sound an awful lot like preadolescence?

> Now all we can see of God is like a cloudy picture
> in a mirror. Later we will see God face to face. We
> don't know everything, but then we will, just as God
> completely understands us. *(1 Corinthians 13:12, CEV)*

Paul describes this transitional time beautifully with phrases like:

- Cloudy picture in a mirror
- We don't know everything
- God completely understands us

How perfect is that? New life stages do feel cloudy, whether we're getting a driver's license, starting a new job, moving to a new home, or watching a loved one die. Seeing life through the blurry haze of change

1

feels uncomfortable because we have to admit over and over that we don't know what's next.

But smile—there's good news. God completely understands. God knows us from top to bottom. God has experienced everything we ever have or will and more. While the kids we lead step from childhood into adolescence, God is fully present to calm their fears (and ours, if we allow it).

Unfamiliar feelings

Anyone who had young children in 2013 saw the movie *Frozen*—possibly multiple times. My favorite character in this blockbuster, Olaf the loving snowman, finds himself at one point separated into three sections and stuck to a wall of snow while being pursued by an ice monster. Olaf vows to help his friends escape by causing a distraction—except that his feet and torso jump down and run off with his friends, and his head face-plants into the snowy ground while he mutters, "This just got a whole lot harder."

When I think about becoming a preteen—or leading a bunch of preteens—that scene sums up my feelings with scary accuracy. We want to protect and guide the children entrusted to us, but we sometimes feel as helpless as a lone snowman's head on the ground. Part of the reason adolescence is so scary is that it's full of changes that are beyond our control, and these changes affect preteens for years to come.

It was during my preteen years that I determined for the first time that I was not pretty. One day in fifth grade, I studied my face and hair in the bathroom mirror, and I didn't like what I saw. Boring hair color, out-of-control perm, fat cheeks, and that one snaggletooth filled the mirror. I left the bathroom dejectedly, and those conclusions are hard to shake, even today.

Being a preteen means experiencing a whole world of thoughts and events for the first time, but definitely not the last. Even as an adult, I sometimes replay that critical inner monologue when I look in the mirror, or worse, see myself tagged in an online photo. (I'm so relieved I did not have to deal with social media as a middle-schooler.)

Preteen years last forever

Preteen years encompass grades four, five, and six, and during these years kids undergo breathtaking changes in hormones, bodies, attitudes, and capabilities. If you're objecting right now because you know that every year of childhood includes major change, I get it. We adults are always exclaiming about how fast time is flying by and how quickly the kids in our lives are changing. So why is this one age-range from fourth through sixth grade so important?

. . . .

Here's why: the new thoughts and experiences that preteens face are lasting. These changes can give permanent definition to their lives.

. . . .

Furthermore, the things we ask for in preadolescence are much more powerful than the things we wanted as children. Preteens don't just beg their parents for something from the toy aisle in the superstore; they beg for their own phone or tablet or laptop, complete with Internet connection to the universe. Preteens don't simply want any old Sunday school room as long as it has toys in it; they want a room with a Wii and comfy seating and as much distance as possible from the nursery. They are capable of more, regardless of whether or not they are ready for more. Choosing which privileges to grant to a preteen is a wizard-level skill to us muggle leaders, and the experiences that those privileges provide can have life-altering effects on these kids.

Social scientists tell us that adolescence begins at age eleven and lasts until age twenty, and those years encompass a process that nobody claims is easy. Eleven to twenty! Children dedicate nine years to coming to terms with new bodies, awakened sexuality, and hormones. Once you have wrapped your head around all that, consider that adults who live and work with adolescents experience a parallel personal revolution. Just as a preteen is learning new ways of thinking and feeling, their leaders now encounter new decisions and doubts. Despite its challenges, this phase provides a unique and short-lived opportunity to begin a transition to a whole and Spirit-filled adulthood.

Nothing is familiar

Do you remember what it was like to be ten? I recall a general sense of confusion as a preteen because everything felt like trial and error—with errors that seemed to far outweigh the trial. My most prominent memory from the age of ten was when my parents took me away for a special birthday weekend, which was actually a huge ruse to trick me into an enlightening conversation about sex. They held me hostage in our hotel room and forced me to look at diagrams of the human body in books with titles like *How Babies Are Made* or *Don't Worry, You're Normal!* It was puzzling.

Everything for a preteen is unfamiliar. Think of your first week at a new job or your first blind date, and imagine having those helpless, lonely feelings without any prior experience to lean on, and that's pretty much what it's like to be a preteen every day. It's no wonder they try to assert power every two seconds. They're desperate to feel some control!

Imaginary audience

The concept of the imaginary audience is absolutely key to understanding how to talk and listen to preteens. These growing kids are eternally in performance mode. For preteens, there is an unseen audience everywhere they go, even when they're in the privacy of their own bedrooms. This imaginary crowd is extremely judgy, and its opinions are based upon the perceived appearance and behavior of peers. When a fifth-grader wears sweats and her hair in a knot on her head to church, you may not be impressed. But you do need to realize that she did not choose that style just because it's comfortable and easy, but because she is playing out a script written by the other peers in her head. This is why preteens flip out when their choices or needs are questioned. They are terrified of getting a poor review from an extremely nitpicky inner crowd.

Preteens, much like adults, confine themselves to what is called a "cultural script" for what they believe is supposed to happen, based upon what their peers are saying or doing. For example, if two of a ten-year-old's peers get smartphones on their birthdays, he will not just expect one as well, he will feel unmoored and lost without one. He longs to follow his script.

But even when preteens put forth their best efforts to please the audience in their heads, it never seems to work. This unforgiving audience continually says to them, "You're not enough," and preteens often take that critique to its logical conclusion: they will never find love. It's shocking for me as an adult to believe that ten-, eleven-, and twelve-year-olds already care about love, but study after study has shown that they do.

So when your preteens rail against your instructions, don't be offended. Their complaints are not attacks on you; they are indicators of fear. You have just caused them to go off-script, and they don't know what their imaginary audience will think about that. It might help to acknowledge to the preteens you lead, "Listen, you guys are super cool and super smart. But the time we spend together isn't about you and isn't about me. It's about God, honestly. Our focus is on God and what God might want to say to us today."

The power of friends

It's a little bewildering to think about how early our kids begin to live for love until we remember that God did design us for community, and one-on-one relationships are the most intimate form of fellowship. But when we are in fourth grade, our concept of intimacy and love is refracted through the lens of our peer relationships, which are not often a great guide for life-giving relationships. It's during this time that kids begin to form friendships for psychological reasons. They choose friends independently, based upon feelings of true kinship and commonalities rather than convenience or their parents' urging.

Influence in friendships often flows only one way. Kids with tendencies toward aggression, disrespect, or disregard for others often influence kids who are generally compassionate and kind. This is one reason why helping our kids navigate friendship is so important.

One night during our church's choral ministry for kids, a leader brought me two sixth-grade boys. They were good, sweet kids with nothing to do that night, so of course they caused trouble. They sneaked into the youth room and stole Popsicles from the fridge, then popped their heads into every rehearsal room just long enough to distract the little kids and bolted away. True delinquents, if I ever saw any.

It took about two seconds to identify which of these ruffians was the instigator and which was the accomplice. I launched into a speech about how they were in violation of the church's insurance policy and Safe Sanctuaries guidelines, how I would inform their parents if there were any further infractions, and how I was going to escort them to Fellowship Hall to assist with the second-grade handbell session, all while failing to hide a smile at their antics. The thing that stuck with me after this pseudo-disciplinary exchange was that it was clear the accomplice boy was uncomfortable even pretending to get into trouble, while the instigator was eating it up. Even though he never would have played pranks at church on his own and doing so was uncomfortable for him, the accomplice didn't speak up to stop his friend. That's typical. The instigators are the influencers.

Preteen boys

There are some gender differences in the ways that preteens navigate this phase, and those differences likely will unsettle you as they do me. Between ages nine to age twenty, the testosterone level in boys increases by eighteen times! Testosterone is responsible for the development of male sexual characteristics, and it also influences feelings of risk-taking, aggression, and dominance. Great googly-moogly—no wonder adolescent boys make dumb choices. Their brains are on hormone overload, which can be exhilarating and overwhelming all at once.

Remember the cultural scripts I mentioned earlier? Those scripts often assign roles to boys based on their physical development. Our culture wants boys to mature quickly, to look and act like grown men as soon as possible. Boys who are taller, bigger, stronger, and heavier than average are well-liked. Peers and adults perceive them to be confident and to possess leadership potential.

This perception is often a self-fulfilling prophecy. As early maturing boys are perceived to be more responsible, they are given more responsibilities and therefore become more responsible (or at least more experienced). These boys also tend to be more stressed out than boys who mature late.

By contrast, boys who are shorter, slower, thinner, and lighter than their peers are perceived to be weak, lacking in leadership abilities, and less worthy of trust. This perception also becomes self-fulfilling, as these boys are picked last for the team by peers and by leaders.

Because our self-concept is typically based upon the real or imagined audience to our lives, we take whatever place in the world these voices assign us. A boy who happens to grow early will often tend to feel good about himself, while a boy whose growth spurt comes later usually experiences depression and low self-esteem during the years between ten to twelve. Fortunately for boys, the depression caused by slow physical maturation will usually dissipate around age thirteen or fourteen, especially once the growth spurt hits.

Leaders, we must not play into these cultural dictates. Learn to "look on the heart" like God does, not at the outward appearance. Don't comment on a boy's stature or weight, and take a long look at whether you treat any boys differently based upon their stature. If you need a group to do some heavy lifting, don't cherry-pick. Invite all the kids to help. When you catch kids in your group discussing who's the strongest or the weakest, put an end to the conversation. In your ministry, endeavor to give every kid a place and a positive identity.

Preteen girls

Hormonal changes for preteen girls are also significant, with estrogen levels increasing by eight times during adolescence. Unlike boys, girls are supposed to develop late, according to our cultural norms. Girls whose bodies grow faster than average are viewed as weak, insecure, and unattractive. We like our girls to be smaller than the boys, with small features and long, straight hair. It's the tall basketball player plus tiny cheerleader archetype. (I realize most places idealize football players over basketball, but I'm from Kentucky.)

For those unfortunate girls who are taller than all the other girls (and boys) in their age group, the consequences to their social standing are often negative. Girls who mature faster than others report feeling depression and self-hatred, and unlike boys, girls hold on to these feelings well into adulthood. While a boy whose growth spurt comes later than normal will eventually shed his depression and regain emotional equilibrium, girls remain critical and negative about their appearance. Women often continue to experience societal pressure around their appearance well into adulthood.

For both genders

Hormonal changes get a bad rap, and I admit that they can't be ignored. However, there is a much bigger factor behind the angst and rebellion we associate with preteens and teens: cultural expectations. These are scripts we wordlessly give our children every day, which they follow to a T. Social scientists find that during middle childhood, the average kid still hangs out in gender separate groups: girls with girls and boys with boys. The only divergents who seem to achieve mixed gender friendships are the very popular and the very unpopular. Have you seen this phenomenon in your church?

Kids gravitate toward friendships with others who are their same size, not necessarily their same age. Girls and boys who mature quickly often are accepted into social groups that are much older than they are. These older friends frequently provide access to drugs, pornography, off-color humor, alcohol, and adult interests that younger children are not developmentally ready to face. Again, the new experiences provided by adolescence can have lifelong effects.

Discrepancies in kids' rates of development can bring them deep shame. This is so incredibly sad because there is nothing that could be more amoral or further from their control! Because they cannot control their developmental rate, they beg for freedom in all other areas. Rather than restricting their freedoms as much as possible, our goal should be to provide opportunities for preteens to earn it.

Leaders of preteens

"Have mercy on us all, Lord, for we know not what we do."

That is our starting point. Let's all just agree that this is where we begin a discussion about "how to minister" with these amazing and enigmatic urchins. Brace yourselves for a wonderful, humbling, fulfilling ride.

Fortunately, we have evidence which helps us understand how power-less preadolescents feel, and knowing that is the key to developing relationships with them. They are going to claw for any possible freedom they can get their hands on, from taking twenty-minute bathroom breaks to interrupting a lesson just to get attention. It's up to us as adult leaders to determine which freedoms they can handle. These choices should be made in advance and consistently enforced.

If you're working with fourth- through sixth-graders in any ministry context, there are three approaches to cultivate from the start:

1. A supportive attitude

2. The mindset of a counselor

3. A healthy sense of humor

Supportive attitude

Kids are changing constantly, and we had better keep trucking right along with them. The biggest difference between working with elementary-aged kids and working with preteens is that with preteens, adults are no longer the only decision-makers. The kind of adult a preteen needs is collaborative, supportive, and understanding. A great preteen leader treats the kids like people with some capacity for self-direction.

When a second-grader asks if he can sit on top of the rickety church basement table to decorate his paper, I respond, "Nope, hop down. It's dangerous up there." When a fifth-grader asks the same question, my response should give him more credit. "Hmmm . . . what do you think could happen if you did that? How do you plan to keep yourself and others safe if the table collapses? Can you think of a better spot?" With preteens, we provide conversation in place of answers. That's what being supportive looks like.

Mindset of a counselor

Working with preteens is also a lot like being a counselor. Every good therapist sees to her clients' safety first. In a counseling relationship, we are safe from fearing the counselor will gossip about what we have shared. Encourage preteens to see you as a safe person, and then demonstrate your trustworthiness.

You are committed to taking the best care of them you can, which means sometimes you will need to share what a preteen tells you with the child's parent, the pastor, or child protective services. Let the kids know where the boundaries are, while making it clear that your goal is their well-being. They can ask you anything, and you won't laugh at them. They can tell you anything, and you will still love them. And no matter what, you will get them the help that they need.

Regularly remind the preteens you lead of these things. Start each school year (or each small-group time) with the same general welcome: "I am here for you all. I'm leading this group because I love you, and I know you can do amazing things. You can tell me anything, and I'll believe you, and I'll help you process it. Sometimes you and I will need to share things with your parents or with a pastor, and sometimes we'll just share it with God. Either way, I've got your back."

Sense of humor

I don't feel like I need to write a paragraph of instructions about having a sense of humor. That seems obvious. So, instead of a few instructive words, let's simply commiserate here, okay? Preteens will test all the limits, just like we did when we sneaked the landline up to our bedroom or swiped twenty dollars from our parent's wallet when we were their age. They'll demand that you treat them like an adult and ask for all kinds of privileged treatment during church activities, and in the next sentence they'll ask you when it'll be time for more snacks and start climbing on the church playground that was designed for preschoolers. If you don't laugh, you'll probably cry. Choose to laugh.

Power plays

The name of the game when working with preteens is **freedom**. They want freedom and power, and we want to keep them safe. The key here is to grant them freedom where it doesn't really matter and retain control on issues that are truly important. In my experience, if preteens feel like they have some room to exercise their own volition, they will accept the other restraints you place on them. This balancing act is never perfected, but goes on to eternity as a constant give and take.

So, what freedoms are all preteens ready for? Here are a few. We should always grant preteens the freedom to:

1. Ask questions about absolutely anything

In this in-between stage of development, with everyone growing at different rates, it's impossible to know exactly what they're thinking all the time unless they tell you. And they almost certainly won't tell us unless we invite them to first.

Younger elementary-age kids are totally concrete thinkers. For them, the correct answer to every question is "Jesus" and the story of Noah's ark is basically just a zoology lesson. They need to have real-life, current examples for us to launch from. We don't go into great depth with most kindergartners about mental illness, death, or romance because those concepts are too abstract for them. Preparing a lesson for kids in elementary school is relatively simple.

Then about ten years later, adolescents live in the abstract. They're questioning their faith, comparing their family's rules to what they see in the world, and making political statements online. Their default approach to conversation is often in the form of an argument. They might even read some nonfiction in middle or high school and enjoy talking about it with adults! Tangible examples are boring to them.

And in between those two groups are our preteens, whose brains are just beginning to venture into abstract territory. They need guides who have already been there and aren't alarmed by exploratory ideas—and if you're reading this book, then you are one of those guides. But five minutes after any philosophical discussion with a fourth-grader, chances are he will be making armpit fart noises again or starting a leapfrog contest in your one-hundred-square-foot classroom. All of this is normal.

There is one fail-proof way to know that a child is ready to start to thinking abstractly, and it is this: when she starts to ask abstract questions.

Here's one thing we've got to get straight, adults. For the preteen who asks questions because of a sincere desire to learn, no topic should be off limits. Where would you rather the children in your ministry learn about sex? friendship? God? body image? drugs? weapons?

. . . .

For at least some kids, the information sources are limited to a trusted adult or Google.

. . . .

If the thought of talking to a ten-year-old about mass killings or pubic hair growth makes you squirm, you're in excellent company. I've had lots of practice, and I still feel an urge to process these kinds of preteen exploration conversations with a therapist afterward. But then I remember that it's either me or an image search on the Internet, and I decide I can handle it. Talking to kids with a straight face about whatever they ask about is called adulting.

During a retreat for fifth- and sixth-graders at my church a few years ago, a flock of girls approached me in the gym during a free period to say they had a question. And what soul-searching, theological, insightful, and sermon-illustration-ready query did they pose?

"Ms. Sarah, um, what's foreplay?"

Let me just tell you, friends—nothing can prepare you for that. I'm convinced the only reason those girls felt comfortable enough to approach me was that my ministry team had just spent the first six hours of the retreat encouraging them to ask questions. Here is a model we all should follow:

- Each week, tell the kids in your ministry that you love them and that they can come to you with any questions.
- Listen when they ask.
- Try not to freak out.

This communication pattern is critical for kids to develop their understanding of the world in a healthy way. If they're asking you about something that you don't think they should know or worry about yet, well, you probably need to answer their questions anyway. We have no idea what our kids hear on the bus or at the lunch table at school. Remember the invisible audience in their heads? When they hear about something for the first time, they're definitely not going to let on to their peers that they are out of the loop. They're going to grab their phones and look it up! The only, and I mean only, possible safe alternative that they have is to talk to a trusted adult. And in most cases, those conversations only happen after encouragement from that adult.

After answering the question matter-of-factly, always ask them if they've talked to their parent(s) about it, and encourage them to do so. And if a child's question causes you to suspect any level of abuse or neglect, report it to your supervisor.

So, in the spirit of making something sound a lot easier than it is, tell them to talk to you about anything, and then answer their questions.

2. Do for themselves

I love this one because I think it hits the sweet spot of relieving the adult from some responsibilities and making the preteen happy to be in charge. Basically, allow and encourage your preteens to do everything that they can possibly do for and by themselves. Here are some examples of things we generally no longer need to do for them:

- Set out and serve food
- Set up chairs before small group
- Pull out all the craft supplies for a project
- Get out and put away equipment
- Walk them to the bathroom
- Mark their names off the attendance list
- Find and read the Bible verse
- Choose a group service project
- Tell them exactly which words to write on a get-well card
- Clean up their trash
- Prepare discussion questions in advance

Note: This list is generic and written for a group of able-bodied kids. Check out Chapter 5 for many more thoughts on ministry with preteens who have disabilities.

These things are simple, right? But it's fun to see how much excitement kids get when heretofore disallowed tasks are opened to them. They love having meaningful work to do and feeling autonomous, and we can give them that gift so many times by reserving as many tasks as we possibly can for them to do on their own. The more you can delegate to preteens, the more open they'll be to hearing about the things they can't yet do.

3. Make jokes

Have you talked to a kid lately? They're hilarious. Some of my favorite moments in ministry are when a sixth-grader has said or done something solely to get a laugh, and it usually works. Granted, sometimes I'm laughing because of the joke and sometimes because the joke was so bad, but no matter—the point is the laughter. Make a joke out of everything you possibly can. Other than conversations about sacred things or safety, almost everything can be lighthearted and fun. Let your kids know that you want to have a good time with them.

Limiting freedom

Before we get too carried away with these wonderful freedoms we can offer to preteens, let's discuss one important limitation we need to keep in place for them (and other adult leaders of preteens). Many of these are things that will be discussed mostly in Chapter 4 when we talk about safety measures for preteen ministry. But while we're talking about their development, let's go over one major freedom that we just can't tolerate with our preteens: judgment and exclusivity.

As kids act upon the cultural scripts they detect all around them, all while venturing from concrete to abstract thinking, they can easily compartmentalize other people based upon outward appearances. We must not perpetuate these cultural scripts for the kids in our ministry areas. We must create a safe space by always holding our preteens to account for cliques, gossip, finger-pointing, name-calling, and stereotyping of any kind. Preteen ministry is a fun place to be, but it has no room for jokes that are racist, classist, ageist, ableist, homophobic, or judgmental of body types. Our preteens do not have the freedom to be hateful, even if they're just repeating something they heard at home.

A few ways to help rewrite these cultural scripts in your ministry are:

- Start every week with a short get-to-know-you activity so that kids learn more about each other than just what they can see on the outside. (See a list of great icebreakers in the appendix.)
- Become famous with your preteens for saying things like, "Every single person has unique gifts from God," or "You are all different in really special ways."

- Practice assigned seating in your class, forcing girls and boys to intersperse and breaking up cliques. Don't always allow best friends to be in the same small group together.

- Firmly but lovingly point out any unfair cultural scripts that you see or hear in your group. When a preteen walks through the door wearing a shirt that belittles any other person, tell her, "You have an amazing sense of humor, and I love having fun with you. But the shirt you are wearing could be hurtful to others, and I know that's not your goal. You can either turn it wrong side out, or I can give you a sweatshirt out of lost-and-found to wear over it."

At the beginning of each new school year, sit down with your preteens and create a covenant together. Let them decide what goes into it, with you asking the guiding questions such as:

- How will we show love to each other this year?
- How will we show love to our leaders this year?
- When someone says something we don't agree with, how will we respond?
- What are our group rules?
- How will we help anyone who breaks the rules to get back on track?
- Which things are absolutely not allowed here?
- What is the best part about this group?
- What do we need to make sure we do every single time we're together?

Recognize and talk about differences in respectful and loving ways. Don't pretend that everyone is the same; teach preteens that the uniqueness of each person demands that we treat people as individuals.

It starts with us as adults. Let's talk to our preteens less about how they look and more about what they think and feel. When we hear them spout cultural norms like, "You're so pretty!" to one another, help them think about what they're really saying and whether or not those words should constitute their highest praise.

16

Other than safety issues that we'll discuss later, preventing hate and bias is the number one restriction to place on preteens.

Setting expectations

We tend to live up to others' expectations of us, whatever those are. That's because we use others' expectations of us as our goal-setting metric and define ourselves by them. If you dread this age group and expect them to drive you crazy, you will get what you expect. But if you choose to love this stage and expect the best out of them, they will rise to the occasion.

The most common attitude our culture takes to preteens seems to be a "throw up your hands in helplessness" approach. I can bet that when you tell a coworker that you're leading a small group of fourth- through sixth-graders at church, their eyes go wide and they start to back away slowly. We assume that we are victims of their surging hormones and can easily feel hurt by their indifference to us or bad attitudes.

But remember—you have the benefit of having already made it through adolescence. You have the wisdom, life experience, and guidance that they desperately need, whether or not they realize it. Don't take their foolhardy objections personally.

Yes, we are their supporters and counselors, but we are also their care-takers and must enforce some rules relentlessly. It helps to give them as much freedom as possible, and it helps to have fun with them and earn their trust. Stand your ground and trust your judgment when they run into your nonnegotiables. Whatever feelings they have about your rules, you know that you're acting out of love.

Final thoughts

As fourth-, fifth-, and sixth-graders begin to think about new things and ask new questions, whole new worlds of Bible study and theological discussions emerge. They can now start to internalize some of those spiritual disciplines like Bible reading and prayer in more adult-like ways, and this growing ability should change the way we approach discipleship with them.

The preteen years can be thought of as the "last chance" period—last chance to shape their friend choices, last chance to construct an understanding of how we treat others, last chance to instill a love of diversity, last chance to celebrate appropriate risks and optimism in the face of failure.

Preteens can still be very literal since they are in a transitional stage between concrete and abstract thinking. I am always surprised when my fifth-graders want to eat goldfish crackers or watch a cartoon movie or carry a doll with them to church, but I shouldn't be. Figuring out how to grow up includes lots of pendulum swings back to childhood and then forward into adolescence. Preteens never stop surprising us.

One thing you can count on, however, is that they'll always see themselves at the center of everything. They have so much to take in during these years that it almost makes sense that they should make everything about themselves. We can use this hubris to help them apply the truths of Scripture to their own lives. We don't just tell them that Joseph was thrown into prison; we ask them to imagine how they would feel in his place. We don't just tell them that Mary washed Jesus' feet with expensive perfume; we ask them what would be going through their heads if they were in that room watching her do that. We give them Scripture, and then see where they take it.

These kids need heroes both real and imaginary. In their next stage of adolescence, they will start to question everything about who they are and what they've been taught. Therefore, don't hold back the good and the bad, but give them real examples of women and men whom they can pattern their lives after. Pull them out of their own heads with stories of Jesus, of missionaries, and of saints.

And as an adult who can commit to loving and leading preteens in a ministry context, you will be their hero too.

CHAPTER 2

EMPOWER

> Israel, listen! Our God is the LORD! Only the LORD! Love the LORD your God with all your heart, all your being, and all your strength. These words that I am commanding you today must always be on your minds. Recite them to your children. Talk about them when you are sitting around your house and when you are out and about, when you are lying down and when you are getting up. Tie them on your hand as a sign. They should be on your forehead as a symbol. Write them on your house's doorframes and on your city's gates.
> *(Deuteronomy 6:4-9)*

People's relationship with Scripture cycles through several phases as they develop. Take a complicated passage like the second Creation story. As children, we hear the story of Adam and Eve, and we believe all of it literally because that is the only approach we have. We're concrete thinkers. It's simple!

When we are older, we begin to develop our own unique identity and ask how the Bible can apply to our lives personally. What does the Creation story have to say about my identity as a man or a woman? Have I been tempted the way Eve and Adam were? Do I feel shame for my sins the way they did? Wasn't it a little extreme for them to be banished from the garden for one mistake?

Then we get older still, and this story becomes even more complex for us when some Old Testament professor rocks our world by telling us that the first few chapters of Genesis look and sound exactly like about forty-eleven other "Creation myths" that were written around the same time. We are now knowledgeable about other cultures and worldviews, and we try to come to terms with biblical passages that were written in a cultural style that feels totally strange to us. We wonder what other parts of the Bible are more symbolic than literal. Wait, do we believe that the Flood happened just like it said? Is the Book of Proverbs even worth reading? How do we feel about the miracles of Jesus?

To this day, I still struggle to interpret the Bible's words in their own context and then apply them to my twenty-first-century life. This is a lifelong task, and each time we revisit Scripture in a new life stage, we're able to dig a little deeper. The journey of interpreting God's Word is a spiraling process—it may feel repetitive, but each time we encounter the same story, we find that it isn't the same as before. Even though the Bible doesn't change, we've changed and grown in the meantime, and those Scriptures apply to our lives in every stage.

That's why Deuteronomy 6:4-9 is such a perfect, timeless set of instructions for people of faith. I am filled with awe that ancient words written to people with an utterly different life experience than mine are so perfectly relevant to this conversation about how parents should raise their children within faith. These three-thousand-plus-year-old words hold the secret of children's discipleship today just as much as they did back then.

These instructions from Deuteronomy are directed toward parents because parents are the primary spiritual influences on the life of a child. They describe the daily, ritualistic, mundane, and repetitive ways that faith is transmitted to children. There's no mention of vacation Bible school or Parents' Day Out programs here, strangely—just the ongoing conversation about God between parents and kids as they stand up, sit down, travel, and arrive. Supporting parents in this at-home spiritual process should be the first bullet point on our ministry leader to-do list.

In this chapter, I'll walk us through some ideas about how to equip parents with empowering, rewarding, and sometimes awkward practices to help them live out Deuteronomy 6. Parents + Church = Team.

Parents are the spiritual ambassadors

The second most frightening moment in my ministry with kids occurred when my supervisor asked me to explain to him the purpose of the children's ministry department. (The most frightening moment was when I wrecked a church bus filled with thirteen rowdy third- through fifth-grade boys, but that's a story for another day.) I was about four years into my full-time role as director of that department, so he had every right to ask this question and expect a thoughtful answer. In the seconds following his question, several options fluttered through my mind:

- Children's ministry teaches kids the stories of the Bible. (*Well, yes and no.*)
- Children's ministry occupies kids so their parents can focus on their own faith. (*Um, no.*)
- Children's ministry makes knowing God fun for kids. (*I mean, not really?*)

The blank stare of panic that I gave in answer didn't seem to surprise my boss at all, for which I am forever grateful. He told me to figure it out and get back to him, and launched me into weeks of soul-searching and study. Brandon, if you're reading this, thank you—this chapter really started on the day you asked me that question.

I have come to be certain about one thing, and it is that parents are the number one source of spiritual leadership for their children.

. . . .

The role of a church's children's ministry is both important and utterly secondary to the religious experiences in the home.

. . . .

The church has a significant part to play, certainly—Deuteronomy 6 said, "Hear, O Israel," not "Hear, O parents!" But if the average preteen attends between one and two hours of structured church activities once or twice a month, that puts them with us a handful of hours each year. Practically speaking, there's just not enough time for the church to produce faithful Christian preteens. For that to happen, the people who are with them at their rising and sitting down and traveling along the road must be in the spiritual driver's seat.

In her book, *Almost Christian,* Kenda Creasy Dean interprets a monumental study of which she was a part called the National Study of Youth and Religion, which collected data from thousands of teenagers about their experience of religion at home and in the church. One of this study's major findings is that teenagers' faith finds its basis in the faith of parents. It is as if a parent's spiritual development acts as a glass ceiling that their kids' faith cannot break through. If parents' own faith is immature and uncared for, it is unlikely that their children's will grow past that point.

In Dean's own words, "Research is nearly unanimous on this point: parents matter most in shaping the religious lives of their children." And, "The best way for youth to become more serious about religious faith is for parents to become more serious about theirs" (p. 112).

If you have served in ministry with children or youth for more than a couple weeks, you have almost certainly already felt frustration at how heavily parents seem to depend on their kids' church experience to make them "good Christians." The reason for this attitude is not because parents are lazy or too proud; it is because their own relationship with Christ is immature, and they simply can't model an in-depth faith that they don't have. To the everyday parent, teaching kids about Jesus is terrifying. I can testify to this from my own life as a parent:

- Last week while I carried a bag of trash out to the can, my son called out to me from where he was playing: "Hey, Mommy, why doesn't God talk to us?" How do you switch gears from your to-do list to theology? I mumbled something about God's speaking to us through others and communicating without actual words, and he shrugged and returned to playing.

- On the way to school, my kids often venture into dangerous philosophical territory, talking about how great it would be to "kill a bad guy" or correcting each other with statements like, "You said you can't do that today, but the Bible says God can do anything, so he can help you." Am I supposed to step in and walk them through these thought processes, or should I just let them play out? And if I do step in, what if I actually make it worse?

- Last December, I realized a week before Christmas that I hadn't had a single conversation with my child about the religious meaning behind Advent or Christmas. As far as my little church staff kid knew, Christmas was a day of receiving presents from Santa. My staff had planned an entire event for church families about the Christmas story, but I personally hadn't touched on the subject at home. Well, shoot.

Ter.if.fying. And yet, it's not a job that anyone outside a child's household can do. Our first job as church leaders is to support parents in their own faith so that they can then pass that faith on to their kids. How much greater impact would we have if we designed children's ministry around the needs and growth of the parents rather than the kids? Too often the church contributes to kids' falling away from faith by focusing on programs for them at church rather than on upholding their parents as primary influencers.

How faith is transmitted

Since parents are the only ones who can effectively disciple their children, we leaders need to understand what the task of spiritual parenting entails. How do parents transmit their faith to preteens?

Step one is that parents must nurture their own spirituality. Don't get me wrong—parents do not need to be professional evangelists to raise their kids to love God! If they did, my kids would be in a heap of trouble. But parents must love God with all their heart, with all their being, and with all their strength, and then live out that love in front of their children. A personal relationship with God results in a lifestyle of faith, and kids need to watch their parents live that way. Referencing Deuteronomy 6, Kenda Creasy Dean urges,

> Note what the Deuteronomist is actually saying here.
> Parents are not called to make their children godly...

> The law called upon Jewish parents to show their
> children godliness—to teach them, talk to them,
> embody for them their own delight in the Lord, 24/7...
> Awakening faith does not depend on how hard we
> press young people to love God, but on how much we
> show them that we do (pp. 119–120).

The point is that kids will get all the spiritual education they need if parents will live out God's work in their own lives. Any other influences (peers, church staff) are bonuses. This belief is based upon social learning theory, the idea that we learn through imitation. Take any child development class, and you will hear about Albert Bandura, the man who spent the 1970s providing evidence that children learn new behaviors (like aggression or empathy) by watching others demonstrate them.

Parents living out their faith in front of their children involves multidirectional conversations about faith. Kids need both to see their dad reading the Bible, hear their mom pray, *and* participate in meaningful dialogue with them about God. God needs to be an open topic of conversation in Christian families, and bringing God into the discussion can start with questions like, "What's your favorite Bible story?" "What do you think Jesus would do in that situation?" and one that my kindergartner often raises, "Is God stronger than the Hulk?"

Study after study shows that teenagers who are devoted to God (and their parents) list faith conversations in the home as the most meaningful and enjoyable part of their religious life.

To sum up everything so far:

1. Parents are the primary faith leaders in a child's life.

2. Parents impart faith to their children through their own faith practices and conversations about God.

3. None of this is possible if parents are not growing in faith themselves.

So how does church support faith in the family?

Bear with me here—I'm about to go all revolutionary on you.

24

If we agree that parents are far and away more effective disciplers of children than church leaders ever can be, and if we agree that parents must be actively growing in their own faith in order to communicate faith to their children, then those of us who love preteens and want to disciple them should coordinate our entire ministry around parents—not preteens. Because the best child-centered church activities in the world will produce nothing more than adults who "went to church as kids" if the parents are not equipped to exemplify and guide their kids' faith day in and day out.

We should accept that terms like "Children's Ministry" and "Youth Ministry" are problematic misnomers. What if we skipped those typical titles and branded ourselves "Parent Ministry"?

. . . .

Our ministry must first consist of strategies to accomplish spiritual growth in parents.

. . . .

When I compare all the hours I have spent researching cool science experiments to use as object lessons or great youth-group games to attract preteens to the amount of time I have spent just talking to their parents, I become overwhelmed. I know how to design a great Bible study or game night for fifth-graders, but talking to their parents about the state of their own souls is daunting.

This is not to say that ministry time spent with preteens isn't worthwhile. They need those positive, safe, loving experiences away from their parents, too, and we can serve as wonderful mentors and guides for them outside the home. It's just that the time preteens spend at church is a tiny sliver of their lives—about one percent. Try structuring your working hours accordingly—one percent of your time planning and preparing for the time you will spend with preteens and the rest investing in the parents who control most of their kids' time. It's especially important to invest in parents now, during the preteen years, because even the parents' time with their children is decreasing—in elementary school, kids spend on average six hours a day with their parents, but in middle school that time will decrease to four hours a day, and in high school it's down to two. We have to help parents take advantage of the remaining time and influence they have before adolescence sets in with all its angst and stress.

You can start with small changes like:

- Begin your youth and children's ministry with adult Bible studies, adult small groups, and adult accountability. Start by asking the parents of preteens where they are struggling in their faith. Collaborate with your pastor of adult discipleship to offer growth classes during every preteen ministry event.

- When you design a retreat or class for preteens, find a great leader who can offer a parent version that takes place at the same place, same time.

- Does someone in your church lead a youth choir on Wednesday nights? Set up a small group for parents at the same time.

- E-mail parents each month to tell them what you're doing and how they can pray over and study the same things the kids are experiencing each week.

Those are baby steps. When you are ready to revolutionize your ministry to increase your impact exponentially, here are some bigger ideas to try:

- Take a red pen to your ministry budget. Allot at least fifty percent of your funds to groups and ministries targeting parent discipleship, not children's programs.

- Offer life-stage accountability groups for parents where they can develop intimacy and provide accountability for one another as they seek to parent faithful kids.

- Pull out your calendar and schedule in-home meetings with every preteen family in your church once a year. Ask parents what they need and how you can support them as they lead at home.

- Go a step further and choose one or two families in your church to disciple in spiritual parenting. Meet with these parents regularly to pray, work through a devotional, discuss strategies for intentional faith conversations at home, and celebrate growth and account-ability. After six months, pair those parents with another house-hold and let them become the disciplers.

• Cancel all annual children's events and explain that you're using that budget money to invest in something more relational, such as a mentorship ministry from older parents to younger parents.

These are just beginnings of ideas. You get to decide the level of risk you're willing and ready to take, but at least start somewhere. For com-plete parent-first models of ministry, look to Chapter 6.

As you delve into parent ministry, it's important to remember that par-ent discipleship is different from parenting education. It is not our job to teach parents how to be good at parenting, and we don't need to have kids ourselves or be familiar with modern parenting strategies to sup-port at-home discipleship. Our task is to invest in the spiritual lives of adults who are parents, to let them know that we are here for them, and that their own faithfulness is the most important factor in their kids' faith development. Don't worry about offering workshops about parent-ing manuals or giving parenting advice. They'll get plenty of that from distant relatives every holiday. We are not trying to develop parenting experts, but rather parents who practice the same spiritual disciplines as every other Christ follower—in front of their kids.

What do we mean by "family" anyway?

When I talk about the family, I try to think of everything that could possi-bly mean—adopted, single parent, divorced, remarried, dual-earner, sin-gle-earner, multiracial, multifaith, intergenerational, traditional, nontra-ditional, healthy, broken, stressed. Households containing two parents are still the most common type, but not by much. In 2015, forty percent of kids under eighteen lived with two married parents, and twenty-six percent lived with only one parent.

The families in our churches are diverse in family structure, socioeco-nomic status, political leanings, size, and every other way. About twen-ty-two percent of kids grow up in families below the poverty line, which means that almost one out of every four kids in our churches does not have sufficient money for basic necessities. In 2014, fifty-three percent of kids identified as white, which means that almost half of the kids in the United States are children of color. According to the American Psychological Association, children of color are at greater risk of less education, less employment, less compensation when employed, more expensive mortgages, greater access to drugs and alcohol, and greater likelihood of mental illness.

. . . .

As you consider how to partner with families in your church, try to avoid making assumptions about the access to privilege families in your church may or may not have.

. . . .

For the purposes of ministry, seek to define families psychologically rather than socially. A family can be any group of one or more adults who take responsibility for the physical and emotional needs of the children in their household. I want to avoid what the experts call "religious familism," the idea that the traditional family is made up of two married adults and two children, and that this family format comprises the best or only social building block for a healthy society. Let's be real. Families are messy, and even the ones with two committed, loving parents have issues.

This means that when Mother's Day rolls around, we don't just make cards for moms; we make cards for all the special women in our lives. We don't give prizes for consistent attendance at church because children of divorce may only be able to come to church every other week at most. We use awkward phrases like, "You can leave when the adult in charge of you comes to pick you up," so that we avoid the assumption that every kid will be claimed by one or more parents at the end of class. And when we know that a child lives with a single parent or that a divorce is underway in a family, we reach out intentionally to each parent separately, whenever possible, to tell them we love them, that we will look out for their children, and that we will communicate with each parent individually whenever needed.

Loving fragile families

Here's where things get complicated. Children's faith develops primarily in the home by observing and interacting with faithful parents. What happens then when that family system is broken or stressed?

Single parents or grandparents who are primary caregivers simply have less time and energy to go around. It's a fact. But they're still their children's best ministers and disciplers, and we church leaders need to figure out how to support every kind of parent and family in that calling. Talk to single parents about their ideas or needs. Use a script such as: "Listen, I am so impressed that you as a single/adoptive/stressed out parent/grandparent/caregiver are prioritizing faith for your kids. I want to support you in any way that I possibly can. How can I make church a stress-free environment for you and your kids? How can I help you incorporate faith into your daily life at home?"

Honestly, the most judgmental conversations I have had about fragile families have been with the staff or volunteers that work with them. It is so, so easy to interpret their consistent late arrivals and seemingly uncaring attitudes as bad parenting. We have got to do a better job of imagining what life is like for families under stress or in crisis. We've got to develop some empathy if we're ever going to support them.

In every church we know kids whose needs for community and mentoring cannot be met completely by the adults in their household. True Christian fellowship means stepping in to be the coaches and mentors and counselors and friends to families who are hurting. Stop and think about whether there are any families in your church who may feel like outsiders. Even if no one is overtly mean to them, families of divorce or single parents perceive judgment. Church needs to be a place where everyone fits. And we make people fit one person at a time.

We are a preteen parent's best friend

It is crazy how many bazillions of support and educational programs for parents of babies and toddlers are out there. This is a good thing! Parents of littles need the support for sure. But parenting preteens presents its own unique and exhausting challenges. Caring for kids who are old enough to sneak out of the house to meet a friend or search the Web to learn more about the phrase they heard on the school bus is one of the most challenging seasons of parenting. So where are the programs for parents of older kids?

You can see what I'm talking about for yourself by doing a quick Google search for "baby and parent (your town here)" and "preteen and parent (your town here)." I just did one for my town of Lexington, Kentucky, and I'm super depressed now. You? I mean, the search results for "baby and parent" is so super sweet, with adorable little music classes and brick-and-mortar stores dedicated to parents of babies. Then I get to the results for "preteen and parent," and I'm filled with fear and dread by ads for therapists, websites for the juvenile justice system, and a news article about a teen and parents killed in a shootout.

This is it, church. This is our in! That gigantic gap between existing programs for babies and for preteens is our slot. We are the ones providing the support networks and education and preventative measures for preteens and their parents. Whether the parents in your church know it or not, you're about to become their best friend. In addition to providing faith opportunities for parents, such as Bible studies and other ongoing adult ministries, here are a few things we've got to do as preteen leaders.

1. Have the hard conversations with parents and volunteers.

Nobody likes this one. Anytime anyone asks what is the most difficult part of leading in a church, this is it for me. Leading uncomfortable conversations with parents, volunteers, or staff drains you emotionally and requires serious prayer and preparation, but it's the most loving thing you've got to do.

Just about every time you are around a group of preteens, something will happen that you'll need to follow up on. Someone will say a bad word or someone will lean so far back in the folding chair that she'll fall out and bang her head or someone will confess that he shoplifted last week or a volunteer will blunder through the definition of "Virgin Mary."

Suddenly, you've got to follow up with parents. As a naturally intense person who hates confrontation, I tend to approach these conversations fully loaded, my head full of the worst possible "what if" outcomes. I put all the pressure of the entire relationship into that one conversation, and it takes on a life of its own. I'd recommend taking a calmer approach.

Logistically, talking with preteen parents is challenging because they don't typically pick up their kids at the classroom door. Preteens are old enough to self-dismiss and may even meet their parents at the car, meaning you never cross paths and must set up an intentional meeting time to see them. Or you can stake out their Bible study room. Or figure out their grocery day and hang in the produce until they show. The stealth level you choose for this meeting is your call. The point is: do not do this over e-mail or text. In person is by far the best, and phone is a far-off second option.

One night about four years later during a youth group-type event for fourth- and fifth-graders, I split the kids into four gender-specific small groups to create skits about the topic of peer pressure. The kids live for these performances, which typically consist solely of cast roles like Mom, Daughter with Bad Attitude, and Friends. This evening, however, the fifth-grade boys provided a real change of pace. As the skit unfolded, my blood pressure slowly rose and my thoughts cascaded:

Wow, these boys look really pleased with their plan. Oh, no—is he a drug dealer? I think there are supposed to be drugs in that bag he's holding. Wait, did he just say COCAINE?!? And now they're all laughing too hard to say their lines. Where are the fourth-graders? Shoot, they're totally paying attention this time. No—no—no—okay, kids under my care just acted out a drug-related shootout. We're never doing skits ever again.

31

It didn't help that my boss's son was a fifth-grade boy in that skit or that a mom of a fourth-grade girl texted me later to ask, "Was cocaine mentioned tonight at church? My daughter just asked me what it was." After talking to my supervisor, we agreed that I needed to say something to the leader in charge of that group. I hung around the fellowship hall between services the next Sunday (stealth level: medium), waiting for him to cross into the sanctuary. When he did, I smiled and waved and fell into step with him, and as we walked I chimed in a manner that I'm sure was way too animated, "Hey, Dave, thank you so much for making small group so fun for those fifth-grade boys. They absolutely love you. After that skit last week, I wanted to make sure you know that you can and should nix any ideas they have that are inappropriate for the other kids. There were some fourth-graders present who didn't know what cocaine was prior to Sunday night, haha. So please know that you're the leader, and you have full power to say no to an idea."

Did you like my use of "haha" humor to lighten a sentence that twisted my whole inside into knots? I thought the "haha" helped.

The leader was a parent of older boys, and he was surprised to hear that some of the content was new information to other kids there. He said a quick sorry, and I smiled and reiterated what a great leader he was for the kids, and we parted ways. He got the main message, and we got to continue partnering together in ministry.

2. Keep parents informed.

If parents do not know what their kids experience at church, we have hamstrung them from building upon it at home. If we design and implement great church experiences for preteens but all parents know about it comes from their observations at drop-off and pick-up, we affirm the misconception that the church will be the primary faith-developer for kids. We usurp the role of parents if we leave them out of the loop.

No matter how you do it, find a way to let parents know what is going on:

- Send a monthly e-mail listing the Scripture, stories, themes, or questions your group is studying.

- If you are studying a particular book or devotional, e-mail families the link so they can buy one for their own homes.
- Start a blog and post regularly about what you're discussing.
- Have the kids journal every week, and send the journal or a copy of it home with parents.
- Invite parents into your space, asking them to serve and observe once a month/semester as helpers so they see what happens firsthand.

Better yet, involve parents in the design of your children's area. Take over their Sunday school class one week and turn it into a brainstorming session. Create a parent ministry team that not only designs but helps to implement ministry to kids during worship services. Meet with families individually each year to get to know them personally and answer their questions about preteen ministry.

3. Create parent milestones for every child milestone.

In Chapter 6, I'll go into more detail about the milestones we can celebrate during these preteen years and why these kinds of celebrations are a great model for ministry, but here I would like to set the stage a bit. One fabulous way to connect with parents in an encouraging, nonthreatening, and empowering setting is by establishing a special event or rite of passage during these preteen years and including a parent component in it.

For example, perhaps your church has an acolyte ministry that begins in fourth grade. This responsibility recognizes that fourth-graders are ready to worship in a new way and that they love to serve. So, when you plan your fourth-grader acolyte training, invite all the parents to a conversation before, after, or during the training.

Or, if sixth grade is the year that the kids in your church transition to youth ministry, then when you begin to kick off the new year (or close out the old one), tell all the parents to come to a parent meeting with you for essential information about this graduation from Children's Ministry.

These milestones for parents can go a ton of ways. If your church is small enough, you may be able to meet one-on-one with families in their own homes or yours. There are also benefits to getting all the parents together in one room at the same time. No matter how you do it, there are a few essential points to cover in each conversation:

- **Listening and commiseration**—Parents of preteens need all the time they can get to vent. If you have more than one household in attendance, ask them to share how they feel about raising a preteen. If they have older children already, ask them to share the most helpful thing they learned from them. Give everyone in the room a chance to realize that they're not alone.

- **Developmental milestones**—Share some of the expectations for this age group that you can find in Chapter 1.

- **What to expect from church for their child**—Go into detail about what their preteens might experience at church under your leadership. Introduce their small-group leaders or your children's ministry team, and allow them to share some of their plans for the year. Share an overview of what themes or Scriptures their kids will explore. Tell the parents how to get in touch with you and what kind of communication they can expect from you. Give them a road map for navigating church with their preteen.

- **What's available at church for them**—Remember, our best chance of developing a true love for God in our church's preteens is by strengthening their parents' faith. Have an adult discipleship leader present to share about any Bible studies or small groups that are open to new members. Give book recommendations to strengthen their own faith. Remind them that, chances are, their kids will grow no closer to God than they are.

- **Blessing**—Pray a blessing over these parents. Commission them to lead their kids through this new stage.

- **Q & A**—Provide a time for questions, either for you or for other parents in the room. Sometimes it helps to pass out index cards and allow parents to write down anonymous questions, then collect them and answer them out loud.

Extra secret: These parent meetings are also a great time for incognito volunteer recruiting. You might slip into your presentation that as luck would have it, there's still one slot left for a fourth-grade small-group leader on Sunday mornings. Or you might go down the parent meeting attendance list the next day and place some calls to people who came but haven't yet found their place of service.

But what about the children?

I realize I have spent a lot of time now seeming to disdain a really good thing—that is, the time spent in ministry with preteens themselves. Please don't get me wrong. High-quality preteen ministries based upon a multiple-intelligences approach, with developmentally appropriate strategies to communicate faith, are of huge value in our churches. After all, we children's directors constantly advocate to make worship and church opportunities more inclusive for kids in an environment that usually caters to only the needs and development of adults. Am I really asking children's ministry staff and volunteers to neglect the kids and focus on adults like everybody else does?

Well, no—and yes. I'm asking you to consider your work as a long game. The time we spend in planned church activities with preteens is important for the current moment, and we should make it as meaningful as possible. But it is the short game. These worship experiences and group activities will impact them today, but when the time comes down the road for them to make their own choices about faith, the fun and significant experiences they had at church will play a secondary or tertiary role in that decision. The way we are raised day to day in our homes is the greatest force in the formation of our personhood and faith up through the preteen years. If we leaders can reach into that world and strengthen the faith influences there, our ministry becomes exponentially more powerful.

. . . .

Putting parents first is the most effective way to put kids first.

. . . .

We have operated too long on an outdated model of children's Sunday school that arose from the industrial revolution, when Sunday mornings were the only time to teach child laborers to read and write by using Scripture. Two hundred years later, we continue to think of children's ministry as an opportunity to educate kids and provide faith opportunities that are otherwise unavailable to them, but this is simply no longer true. In the process, we have encouraged parents to outsource their discipleship role to us and assumed more responsibility than we can handle. These endeavors are not our primary directive any longer.

It still takes a village

Remember, it is the whole church's responsibility to help one another raise faithful kids. While any family scholar can tell you that the family is the most effective and important context for a child's faith development, we can't neglect the importance of the church community too. Studies have shown that while parental nurturing is essential for emotional wholeness, coaching and mentoring by nonparental figures is essential for more external achievements. Our parents' love develops in us identity and wholeness of personhood, but we need teachers and coaches and leaders outside our home to help us discern our vocation, find motivation to do hard things, and achieve success. Parents provide the base, and other leaders provide the direction.

One study showed that while a mother's faith is a great predictor of a child's own faith, an even greater predictor was the frequency of church attendance by the child's peers during adolescence. Church provides peers and trusted adults to help support a child's faith. And as preteens prepare for adolescence, the stage in which peers exceed parents in their influence, establishing healthy friendships with other faithful kids is a winning strategy. Church is where many families find those friends.

But beyond peer relationships, adults that will pour themselves into the lives of someone else's children and display their own faith in front of them are pure gold. There is a richness and depth in nonparental relationships that kids cannot get from their parents alone. You do not need to be a parent in order to lead kids, and in fact, I'd give my back teeth to have a preteen ministry team that consisted of mostly young adults and senior citizens—they are the absolute best.

According to the National Study of Youth and Religion, church involvement is the second greatest factor in an adolescent's faith. There is nothing deterministic about parenting! Even a parent who does everything with absolute perfection (which never happens) can raise a child who turns his back on God.

. . . .

Church community is a safeguard, a buttress, a fortification to help protect and solidify a child's love for God and for herself.

. . . .

I'm so grateful for the day that I met Kevin, a precious third-grader who came to church with his aunt. He was bright and clearly taking everything in, and he threw himself into every aspect of worship that day. Over the next few weeks, he begged his aunt to keep bringing him, and she did. What he wasn't finding at home or at school, he found at church. He was enveloped in a safe, loving, community of worship.

A few months later, Kevin's aunt could no longer bring him because of health reasons, so he convinced his mom to come. Every week he literally brought his mom to church. Pretty soon, we scooped her up too—she became a member of the choir, joined the Children's Ministry Team, and is a friend of mine to this day. All because a third-grader and a church fell in love.

Parents + Church = Team

Preteen years are just limbo, forever feeling in-between. Full-scale impulses and hormones of adolescence are still on the horizon, just beginning to crop up like the first dimness of dusk. And somehow, every time a new trigger or emotion pipes up, both the parent and preteen are surprised. It's all new. But we ministry leaders won't be surprised.

That's what can make us the greatest asset to preteen families—we can help normalize this process and provide a safe and consistent landing zone for parents and kids alike.

CHAPTER 3

MENTOR

Now the boy Samuel was serving the LORD under Eli.
(1 Samuel 3:1)

Samuel, the first great prophet of ancient Israel, was birthed from the prayers of his mom, Hannah. She was unable to conceive, and this inability was a cultural curse that embarrassed her and left her feeling empty and useless. Hannah took an opportunity one day to go to the temple to cry out to God for a son, promising to dedicate the boy to God's service. Sure enough, Hannah conceived Samuel almost immediately. With a mixture of joy and sorrow, she gave her young son to the priest, Eli, to serve in the temple and train to become a priest.

That backstory is important—don't forget Hannah, the parent who committed her child to God's work. But the real story begins when Samuel is a preteen, twelve years old, on the cusp of adolescence. He has spent his entire life with his mentor, Eli, learning how to care for the temple and serve the Lord. Then one night,

> The LORD called to Samuel.
> "I'm here," he said. Samuel hurried to Eli and said,
> "I'm here. You called me?" *(1 Samuel 3:4-5)*

But Eli hadn't called, so Samuel figured he must have imagined it and went back to bed. This happened two more times. Eli finally realized that God must be speaking to Samuel, so he gave him instructions:

> Go and lie down. If God calls you, say, "Speak, LORD.
> Your servant is listening." *(1 Samuel 3:9b)*

Samuel obeyed, and when God spoke again he responded as Eli had instructed. God then communicated some hard truths to Samuel, telling him that Eli's grown sons would soon be punished for cursing God with their words. God said Eli had known about this behavior but hadn't addressed it, and therefore no amount of apologizing or sacrificing would bring reconciliation. The next morning, Eli asked poor Samuel to convey this awful message. And knowing that it was right, Eli accepted it.

I love that we get a sneak peek into a literal calling story right here in Scripture! This is a real gem—a concrete moment of God's calling out to a kid and setting him on a life path of delivering God's messages. My reading of 1 and 2 Samuel tells me that Samuel continued to hear from God all his life, just like this first time. Hearing and sharing God's words became Samuel's life work.

The Bible is absolutely teeming with other stories of young people hearing calls from God—David, through the prophet Samuel several years later; Joseph, through dreams about stars and wheat; Mary, from an angel who appeared to her visibly; Josiah, through the reading of God's word; and even young Jesus, through conversation with theologians.

Very few of us discern God's call in isolation like a monk on a mountainside. For most, calling comes as a concert of voices that harmonize over the course of years and relationships and experiences.

Just as Samuel grew up in God's house and heard God's voice clearly there, our preteens should be able to sense God's presence in their lives most clearly through the relationships and belonging they find in our churches. God calls everyone, but it is our preteens who are poised to hear that call with an openness and sense of preparation that only middle childhood can afford.

My calling story

At the risk of discrediting myself, I will tell you that I was homeschooled from second grade through high school. All those homeschool rumors you've heard about counting chores as "math" and using romance novels to teach literature—they're true, but only for a small subset of homeschoolers. My tyrannical parents held family devotions no later than 7 a.m. each day, and classroom time started at 8 a.m.

My parents' decision to educate me at home was the beginning of God's speaking a calling into my life. I read voraciously and spent lots of time learning to communicate with people of all ages. Around sixth grade, a hairy time for anyone (in more ways than one), I felt completely odd and out of place among my peers at church. My understanding parents and an overworked/underpaid children's ministry director, Annette, agreed to let me assist in the nursery rather than attend Sunday school. And so it began.

Soon, I was promoted and given the pretend title, "Children's Ministry Coordinator." This was genius on Annette's part because it kept me away from the liability of hands-on work with babies, and it freed her up to do everything else. I monitored the halls, checked in with teachers throughout the hour, ran errands, fetched craft supplies, delivered messages, and strutted the halls with a sense of importance and empowerment filling me head to toe. My family never missed church, so I was a consistent volunteer—basically a gold gem for any ministry director. For a couple of years, this was my place of belonging.

A couple of years later, a new Children's Ministry director in a moment of desperation asked if I would teach the fifth-grade Sunday school class. Yep, that's right—just a few years out of fifth grade myself, I found myself teaching this group that no one else could be found to lead. I recall trying to be funny at times so they'd like me, and I also remember writing and teaching my own series on modesty. Moral of the story: Don't let middle-schoolers teach fifth-graders. For so many reasons.

Soon after that, my family became missionaries to Russian children, serving two years in a school in Indianapolis and then spending what would have been my senior year of high school in Moscow. During that year, I once again benefited from a volunteer shortage and was given the privilege of leading children I wasn't qualified to lead. Misha and Nikita, both age seven and speaking not a lick of English, became "my kids" five days a week for nine months.

Back in the States after that year, I began to think about attending college in the fall. My parents have always understood the importance of calling, and they made a deal with each of us kids that they would fully fund our college education as long as we knew what we wanted to do with it afterward.

I remember as clearly as yesterday, riding in the back seat of the van that summer, asking myself what I wanted to do with my life. All these experiences rolled through my mind in waves, and in an inspired moment I just knew. Everything in my life so far led me to my calling: to serve and educate parents as they seek to raise whole, healthy, God-loving kids. It all began when a church leader gave me a role and allowed me to use my gifts as a preteen.

What is calling?

There are two levels of calling, both interconnected but not quite equal. Chapter 2, in fact, said just about everything I can say about primary calling. The first calling of all God's children is to love and obey God day to day. Scripture pulls us into God's arms over and over and over again, and this call is inclusive and the same for every person.

> Desire first and foremost God's kingdom and God's righteousness, and all these things will be given to you as well. *(Matthew 6:33)*

> *You must love the Lord your God with all your heart, with all your being, with all your mind and with all your strength. (Mark 12:30)*

Anyone who responds to this first calling on all our hearts will find everything else fall into place. And whose responsibility is it to open the ears of preteens to hear this first call? Parents! Those in a preteen's household. Remember the work that Hannah did as mother to Samuel. She prayed for him, and she approached his life as a service to God. While I do not propose that every parent leave their firstborns on the church steps to be trained in God's service (please, no!), I do love that

Hannah introduced Samuel to God by placing him in God's house. Her actions are an (extreme) example of how all parents should nurture in their children this primary calling of loving God.

It is the secondary calling that I want to focus on here in this chapter, a divine invitation to a specific vocation or ministry based upon the gifts and passions that God has implanted in every child. Secondary call is a personal application of the primary call. I am not talking about career coaching for preteens here. Please don't misinterpret this chapter as my advocating for setting kids on a course for professional success and comfortable retirement.

. . . .

God created everyone with a desire to make a difference in the world, and God equips everyone just a little bit differently than everyone else. This is the second calling.

. . . .

Second calling: our passion meets the world's need

In a paper directed toward career counselors for adults, some highly educated scholars have given "calling" three aspects:

1. It is a "transcendent summons" that

2. gives purpose to your life and work, and is

3. primarily motivated by helping others.

Your vocation, then, is the actual work you do, whether paid or volunteer, to live out that calling. These secular scholars also note that interpreting our calling is an ongoing process, not a one-time sign in the clouds that we then blindly pursue the rest of our lives.

A definition I like even better is Frederick Buechner's claim in *Wishful Thinking*: "The place God calls you to is the place where your deep gladness and the world's deep hunger meet." This includes everyone because God calls everyone. We do not always answer, and we might not always even hear, but the calling is there. In fact, one of the greatest frustrations I think we feel as adults is that we have not discovered our meaning in life. Do you know someone who is in a job he hates or is vocationally paralyzed? Feeling our innate, human longing for purposeful work but having no idea how to go about it is debilitating.

We assume a false dichotomy between people who do "normal" work and people who are called to do God's work. Most of us, when asked what our calling from God is, would not include relationships with friends, Bible study, participation in church community, and our everyday battle against injustice, but in fact all those things are parts of God's call on all of us. Even though a heavenly megaphone has not blasted through the clouds to bestow a spiritual office upon you, you still are called.

We discover our second calling through a combination of four factors:

1. Talents—What are your best gifts? What do you enjoy teaching others about?

2. Experience—When in your personal history have you felt the most passion? Which experiences have impacted your personality or prepared you for something bigger?

3. Prayer—As you seek God, how does God direct your steps? Whom does your heart beat for?

4. Mentoring—What do trusted coaches and friends tell you about your gifts and need for growth?

While parents can and should speak to these factors in their preteen's life, the church provides a broader and more objective context in which to explore each of them. Parents are not mentors—they're parents. Preteens need other adults to mentor them and pray for them, and they learn more about their talents and have wider experiences through group activities with peers.

Mentoring a preteen's call

In the discernment process, a third-party mentor is a key player. When there is a problem to solve or a truth to find, an objective outsider who loves and supports the parents and the preteen can see and say things that others can't.

As church leaders, we must take responsibility for helping kids identify and practice God's call on their lives. We get to create success scenarios for them to live out, and no matter where their later careers or hobbies take them, they will not forget these wins from their preteen years. Mentoring a preteen in calling is a privilege.

One way that I have tried to do this is to call out a child's gifts publicly whenever I have a chance. And as luck would have it, usually it's those kids who don't fit the mold—who interrupt every prayer and pull their sweaters over their heads while you're talking to them—who are the ones who give us the most opportunities to identify their gifts.

I know a second-grader who will do anything to make people laugh, including create constant distractions during Kids' Worship. Inwardly, this can drive me up the wall. But when I am my best self, I can say, "Hey, Sam, you have the amazing gift of joy. You make other people laugh! I love that. I'm going to make a deal with you: You have sixty seconds to use your gift of joy in any safe way you want. Make us laugh until our tummies hurt! But when your sixty seconds are up, I want you to promise not to distract others from worshipping Jesus the rest of the time, okay? And if you keep your promise, you can have another sixty seconds at the end of Kids' Worship. Because laughter and joy are definitely part of worship too!"

. . . .

The behaviors that feel like distractions and inconveniences may be manifestations of unique gifts that a child wants to contribute.

. . . .

In my last seven years of ministry, I can think of three preteen girls who have all evidenced a singular connection with the holy. When these girls speak up, it's as if they are interpreting God's Spirit without even trying. When I would share a New Testament verse with a group of fifth-graders, Lily would pipe up with something like, "That makes me think about how God loves us so much that God has placed angels all around us to keep us safe and be our friends." I will never forget talking to some kids about Noah's ark and feeling my heart swell when Maddie wrinkled her brow, raised her hand, and stammered, "But . . . how could God leave all those people outside the boat to die?" One of my favorite kids of all time, Lisa, hides the Bible in her heart like nobody's business. You want Bible facts? She's got 'em. You want to have an actual conversation about a Bible story? She's in. When Lisa's mom informed her that she planned to attend a women's Bible study, Lisa became so jealous that she guilted her mom into creating the church's first ever Bible study for third- through fifth-grade girls. Lisa recruited another adult leader and mapped out the study outline for the first six-week session.

When you encounter these kinds of interactions, name them for what they are—the work of God's Spirit in their lives. Every one of those three girls has tired of hearing me say, "Wow, girl, you have a gift. Thanks for being our theologian-in-residence today."

As a staff person who oversees broad ministry areas, I don't have many opportunities to step into a one-on-one mentoring role with a preteen myself. Rather, I help them identify a fitting mentor and then oversee the mentor-mentee relationship along with the parents. It is not hard to ask an adult to accept the privilege of shaping a preteen's trajectory toward faithful work—what an honor!—but it is a big ask. Can you think of a more literal application of the United Methodist baptismal covenant?

> With God's help we will proclaim the good news and live according to the example of Christ. We will surround these persons with a community of love and forgiveness, that they may grow in their trust of God, and be found faithful in their service to others. We will pray for them, that they may be true disciples who walk in the way that leads to life.

Why the preteen years?

While I am not sure if Erik Erikson's famous theory of psychosocial development is always helpful, I find his take on elementary and preteen years to be spot on. He calls this stage Industry vs. Inferiority, which is a time for taking on new projects and exploring bigger ideas, but also enjoying the simpler tasks and joys of younger years. Kids at this age long to feel competent to complete meaningful work, and if they don't have any opportunities to create meaning or if they feel they have failed at their efforts, they will have no inner purpose to lean on during turbulent adolescent years and highly pressured young adult years. This is the period for beginning the discernment process with them.

They have completed those early elementary years where the biggest goal was to learn to read and sit still and participate in a social group. Now they are learning specialized skills in choirs, on basketball teams, and at science camp. During the middle and late elementary years, kids develop a sense of what they're good at and what they're not, accompanied by either pride or shame.

At this point in a preteen's life, an adult who knows them well can easily identify multiple skills, gifts, and unique experiences that make him the person he is. That is the start of discerning God's call! It's all about combining experience with skills and then creating intentional spaces for the person to experiment within that skill set.

Apprenticeship

In my church, we call this process for preteens Apprenticeship. After graduating from Kids' Worship, fourth-grade kids meet with me and their parents to have a conversation about their likes, dislikes, talents, dreams, and experiences. We identify a role in the church where the preteen can begin to serve, match them up with a mentor who is already leading in that area, and let the pair work together for a school year.

Currently, the most faithful volunteer in our church's nursery ministry is Eleanor, a fourth-grader who chose caring for babies as her place of ministry for this year. It is almost comical to watch how heavily the staff and volunteers in the nursery rely on Eleanor. She arrives early every week, greets every child at the door, knows whose diaper bag is whose, and is a whiz at calming any baby with separation anxiety or playing quietly with a child who doesn't connect well with the others.

Her mentor is a young adult who has worked in the nursery for years also and is now an elementary schoolteacher, and together they have made a list of all the goals they want to achieve during this year's apprenticeship. Eleanor not only has a place of belonging in the life of the church, but she is building skills that she will use the rest of her life. God is using this time of serving to make her into the minister she is meant to be. (Please do not fret, those of you who see all the red flags going up about a ten-year-old in the nursery. She is always supervised by two adults, does not change diapers, and is well aware of her status as a helper, not a leader. She also attends worship every week after her nursery shift.)

These special, sacred years are the perfect moment emotionally, developmentally, and socially to dive into conversation about God's calling. They can tell us what they love and what they don't, and they can demonstrate the things they excel at—gymnastics, cupcake decorating, water sports, horseback riding, sound mixing, Legos, love for animals, reading, anything—no interests are off limits. God uses it all! And they want to make it count for something.

Church is the practice field for calling

Even adults would benefit from seeing church as a safe place to practice living out their faith, but this is especially true for our preteens. Our churches should be places where preteens know they fit because they always have a role or a job to do there. In early elementary, kids may be comfortable coming into a small-group room and just having a good time, but by the age of ten those same kids now need a better reason to be there. They are beginning to understand themselves in new ways and entertain new dreams, and if the church doesn't create space to live out those passions, they will find another place to do it, or worse, never realize that God has a job for them to do at all.

If possible, consider reorganizing your preteen ministry every year based upon the gifts of the kids who are in it. Start the year with a bare bones outline for the morning, leaving room for flexibility and alterations. As you pick up on kids' personalities and talents, employ them.

The boy who never talks or makes eye contact? Find a time to ask him privately if he will handle administrative tasks for the group like taking attendance, setting up or tearing down chairs, taking notes that can be e-mailed out later, writing prayer requests on the board, or writing notes of encouragement to the other kids. The girl who never shuts up, especially when there is the slightest opportunity to push the limits of appropriate topics? Script a prayer (or have the group collaborate to write a prayer) that she can read or recite each week at the beginning, providing her with a visible leadership role and a speaking part that contributes to others' discipleship. Is there a kid who arrives early every week? Have that kid set out snacks or write the week's verse on the board or turn on all the sound equipment.

. . . .

The point is to find something unique about every child, point out that unique skill in a positive way, and channel it into purposeful work that benefits the whole group.

. . . .

In my ministry, I insist that once I have doled out a particular responsibility to a preteen, no one else is allowed to have it. The roles are as unique as the persons who play them, and if that person is absent one week, it is appropriate for everyone else to feel the loss. If a child asks, "Hey, Smith isn't here so can I write on the board this week?" the answer is no—the board will remain blank this week. Not because another child wouldn't do a great job, but because the work we give to preteens secures for them a place within the ranks, and that place must be protected at all costs.

Scholars who study transitional periods in children's lives talk about the idea that children are never just receptors for adult goals and instruction. Rather, they are reciprocators who should be involved in creating meaning for themselves and for the adults in their lives.

Just like adults, preteens will not believe us when we say they are important members of the group unless they can contribute to the welfare of the group. That drive that kindergarten through third-graders have to do things rather than just watch things has not quite worn off yet when they hit fourth, fifth, or even sixth grade. By giving them something to do, we accomplish so many things at once!

1. Fulfill our baptismal covenant.

2. Attract them to return to church.

3. Nurture God's call on their hearts.

You guessed it—that third one is my fave.

Getting creative

It is no lie that I am urging you here to do something that is highly subjective. To take a few interactions with a preteen, base a gifts assessment on those encounters, and harp on it for a year is not just daunting, it is perhaps reckless, right? I do not mean to heap upon you the responsibility for correctly discerning God's path for each preteen in your church. It is not our responsibility to direct them into their exact vocational path, which is disappointing for me but probably good for them. If I could dictate every one of my preteen's vocations, I would send them all to work on developing self-driving cars because I super want one. And now we see why God hasn't delegated this job to me.

We do not predict a child's future or even hit on that child's primary driving passion, and that is okay. But there is power in looking a preteen in the eye from the position of an adult church leader and saying, "Wow, your ability to _____ blows me away. God is really going to use that gift someday!"

The impact of pointing out a preteen's strength and then making space in the church for that strength to shine week in and week out will follow that child forever. God can use every meaningful church experience for good. We simply have to create the spaces. The keyword here is "create."

A ministry that convinces preteens that God has work for them to do and empowers them to practice that work is going to look and feel awkward in many ways because it will be structured entirely around a group of wobbly, immature, heartfelt kids. You may have to rack your brain at times to find any productive participation for the kid who arrives twenty minutes late every week or the one who struggles with a learning delay or everyone's favorite: the entitled, know-it-all pastor's kid (two of them are mine, so I can say that). These "problem children" are exactly the ones who will thrive most with a role to play and a job to do.

Ask the right questions

Have you ever thought about the expectations we set by the questions we ask kids?

"Where do you go to school?"

"What do you want to be when you grow up?"

"How many kids do you want to have?"

Kids are like a seven-foot-tall person—when I see someone that tall, my first question is, "How tall ARE you?" But it's not the first time that person has answered that question. In fact, a guy who is seven feet tall likely answers that question ten times a day. It is old and worn out. We treat kids in the same way, I think, by all of us asking them the same questions. Over time, they translate these interrogations into expectations.

"Where do you go to school?" = "You should like school."

"What do you want to be when you grow up?" = "Your identity is defined by your job."

"How many kids do you want to have?"= "All Christians marry by 25 and have children."

Some cultural philosophers have countered these questions before, like Jaime Casap, Google's Global Education Evangelist. He warns that questions about what kids want to be when they grow up have "no relevance anymore." He continues, "We need to ask students, 'What problem do you want to solve?'"

This question gets much closer to the idea of calling, but it is still not enough in isolation. We need more questions to prompt children to learn to identify as God's children and think about the things that bring them passion and joy. Here are a few questions to add to your preteen conversation data pile:

"Which activities do you love so much that you could do them for hours?"

"What are your favorite things about God?"

"If God were here, what do you think God would say to you?"

"Name two things you do so well that you could teach someone else."

"What are you proud of?"

"Who are your heroes and why?"

Whether kids know how to answer these questions or not, the discussions and activities that we provide them at church should help them explore these sorts of ideas. And for preteens, one of the best ways we can help them discover their passions is through serving.

Importance of service projects

There is no joy quite like that of helping someone else. The mixture of pride and learning intoxicates both young and old, and brings together both the cool and the uncool on an equal playing field. We might not succeed in pulling every child into a vibrant group discussion or meet every kid's unique intelligence with our curriculum, but I have never met a preteen who failed to perk up when a meaningful service opportunity presented itself. Part of the beauty of serving is that we find ourselves in service to others. When we give of ourselves, we discover our own weaknesses and strengths.

The tricky part lies in finding the perfect intersection of safety and capacity for preteens. They are capable of more than they ever have been before! But they are still dependent on adults for the details. They can't wield hammers at a Habitat for Humanity site yet or organize a craft closet without help. In the final chapter, I will present Apprenticeship in detail as a viable and meaningful way to provide supervised serving opportunities for preteens. This ministry model is designed to help individual preteens understand their gifts in a church context under the guidance of a mentor. But for a group of preteens, group service projects are a superb option.

Here are a few age-appropriate ideas to consider:

• **Housewarming gifts**—if your church participates in any home-building ministry, have your kids make housewarming gifts. Decorate dish towels, make stepping stones out of mosaic tiles and cement, buy some inexpensive wood baskets/wall plaques/coat hooks at a craft store and have your kids paint them. Write notes or make a banner that says, "Welcome home!" On the home dedication day, invite the preteens to attend, meet the homeowner, and give the gifts. Or, ask the project leaders if you can bring your preteens to the site on a non-work day and let them write Scriptures and prayers on the studs and floors of the house before they are covered.

• **Research & writing assignments**—by and large, this age group can write and spell adequately, and they can wrangle information from the Internet better than many adults can. If your church is contemplating a new ministry area or adopting a new partner, give your preteens the task of researching it. Put them in groups, give each group a smartphone or tablet (borrowed from leaders), and provide a list of questions to be answered. Let preteens report their findings however they want—slideshow, video message, oral report, written report, drawings, or any other way! Possible questions include:

1. How did this organization start?

2. What kind of help do they need the most?

3. What could our church do to help meet those needs?

· **Internal ministries**—select a few regular Sundays to put preteens to work in the life of the church. Coordinate with head ushers, the hospitality team, nursery staff, worship design, maintenance, and adult classes. Pair preteens up and put them to work in these areas of the church, then pull them out fifteen minutes before the service ends to debrief their service times, ask them how those areas could be improved, and what they learned. Of course, make sure that all preteens are supervised the whole time by adults.

· **Sit at tables**—our church provides a meal one night a week for about twelve men in our city. We sit around tables to eat and share and laugh and listen for an hour before they go to sleep in another building we own. Preteens should have opportunities to sit around tables and put faces to issues they hear about abstractly, like homelessness or aging. If your church has any connection to the community that includes a meal or just conversation time, such as tutoring or nursing home visitation, prepare your preteens and help them to sit and form relationships with people who are different from them.

· **Choose your own projects**—if you have a tightly knit preteen group, allow them to develop their own service project at the beginning of each school year. You may provide guidelines, but let them make suggestions, and write every entry on a board. Then help them make their service dreams a reality throughout the year.

Teaching habits

In addition to serving, there's one other major practice that is critical during this preteen self-discovery period. Spiritual habits contribute to our sense of self every bit as much as acts of service do. Capitalize on their ability to read, write, and report by introducing what we adults call spiritual disciplines. Explain that spiritual habits are the tools we use to build our relationship with Jesus. We make friends by spending time together, finding mutually enjoyed activities, asking questions, learning, and listening. Our relationship with Jesus grows the same way!

As a group, talk through some different Bible reading plans and studies. Do a Bible study together, and help them identify when they can read Scripture on their own at home too. Consider giving (or asking a church member to donate) a set of Bibles to the group so that everyone has the same one. Make sure your room at church contains several Bibles for kids to grab if they don't have one.

Bring in adults from your church who can share their own testimonies of seeking God. Ask church members of every age bracket to share with your group what their practice of spiritual habits looks like on a daily or lifelong basis.

Practice praying for each other and for your own selves with the group. Give them journals and provide time to journal at church, encouraging journaling at home. Talk about the difference between intercessory prayer and personal prayer. Set the goal that by the end of the year, every kid will have led the group in prayer at least once. Pair them up and ask them to exchange prayer requests and then pray for one another. Turn on peaceful music, send them all off into private corners of the room (behind the door, under the table, wherever), and give them time to journal, to read the Bible, to whisper a prayer, or just to be in God's presence. Lead them in lectio divina or other forms of meditation on Scripture. As a group, choose an activity or a luxury food item to fast from. Model for them what confession looks and sounds like, and share with them your own reasons for attending corporate worship.

None of these activities is flashy, and none of them require a modern preteen-centric environment or a young, hip leader. Still, shouldn't we spend our limited Sunday morning influence exposing them to a range of life skills that will draw them into closer relationship with Jesus rather than in anything else? I think of it as doing parents a favor—while it is the parents' responsibility to instill spiritual habits and direct preteens to God day in and day out, we can contribute by showing them new, interesting, fun, and maybe unique ways to connect with God as a group.

Stress and extracurricular

Want to break your heart? Listen to a preteen or adolescent talk about how stressed out they are all the time. Pressure from school, parents, friends, sports, music, performances, and inner voices is amped up in the world of preteens. By the time they get to high school, their performance load is literally unsustainable, but it starts in the preteen years.

I can't count the hours I have spent bemoaning the church's loss of Wednesday night and Sunday morning participation by families who choose sports or rehearsals instead. Our programs suffer and often die at the hands of lacrosse and field hockey. Honestly? It's fine. In fact, maybe those outside activities bless us in disguise. God never commissioned us to go into all the world and make more programs. When we grieve over a kid who misses church camp to play volleyball, we play the role of decision-makers in that family's life. We set ourselves up in competition with all the other activities that families need to give time to. It is time to stop competing with basketball practice and to start helping families consider the purpose and opportunity within all their many environments.

∙ ∙

Instead of guilting families into church-based alternatives, help them serve God wherever they are.

∙ ∙

Who are we to say that God prefers kids to seek the Spirit only within our twenty-first-century church buildings? By positioning ourselves as an alternative to the daily activities of families, we contribute to the stress and confusion they feel about where God wants them to be. Our goal is that every family follow God's path for them, and we don't decide what that is. But we can show them the markers—where their kids find joy and practice their gifts in service to God and others.

Let's make church a place of peace, a haven from stressors that pre-teens feel elsewhere, a place where they learn how to make sense of all their other contexts. At church, we ask kids about their favorite activities and best accomplishments, and then we say, "Wow, isn't it great that God made you that way? I am so proud that you can serve God there. Just imagine what might be next for you!"

Final thoughts

In case you were wondering, this chapter has required a soundtrack while I have written it. Every word I have written, sitting in my pajamas at 6 a.m. with coffee and unpaid bills next to me, is accompanied by the soundtrack from *Moana,* which you should absolutely find a way to watch right now if you haven't already. It's the story of how a young woman is called to an unknown adventure. With the support of a mentoring adult, her grandmother, she sets out across the ocean, following her calling with both fear and passion.

When I hear Moana's song, "How Far I'll Go," I tear up. In fact, I have cried so many times over this chapter I can't count them all. There's so much at stake and so much potential in this short time! I've had difficulty diffusing my intense feelings about calling into sensible and concrete words. This stuff is important. It is a privilege. And for some of you, part of your adult calling could entail mentoring a preteen in her first years of listening to God's invitation.

Here's what I want you to do. Start listening for calling stories all around you. When a college athlete is interviewed after a game or your pastor shares a personal story from the pulpit, look for hints of experience, mentoring, skills, or prayers in their childhood that contributed to the person they are now. Our preteens are works in progress, and we have this short window to be a part of their story. What a huge honor!

CHAPTER FOUR

PROTECT

How does God feel about kids? Scripture is clear; we can argue about a whole lot of verses in the Bible, but I hope I never hear anyone try to convince me that God is anything less than crazy about children. Check it out:

> The disciples came to Jesus and asked, "Who is the greatest in the kingdom of heaven?" Then [Jesus] called a little child over to sit among the disciples, and said, "I assure you that if you don't turn your lives around and become like this little child, you will definitely not enter the kingdom of heaven." *(Matthew 18:1-3)*

> As for whoever causes these little ones who believe in me to trip and fall into sin, it would be better for them to have a huge stone hung around their necks and be drowned in the bottom of the lake. *(Matthew 18:6)*

I do a double take on this passage every time to make sure I'm reading God's Word and not a script from *The Sopranos*. Never does Jesus sound so much like the Godfather as when speaking of the punishment for people who harm children. This is serious business.

Children are VIPs in God's kingdom. These smarty-pants, mess-making, sleep-forsaking, dirt-seeking, short people are God's greatest gift to the church. The very least we can do is ensure that when they are in our care, we protect them. And for preteens, this looks just a little different than it does for younger elementary or for adolescents. Their in-between-ness produces some specific needs and calls for unique safeguards on our part.

Keeping preteens safe is the bedrock of our ministries. Before we can explore ministry models or gush about the programs that draw hundreds of kids every Sunday night, we have no choice but to make certain that we have done everything we possibly can to make church a safe place for them.

My worst day

The day of ministry that haunts me the most is the one time I had to call the Department of Social Services, or CPS as I still call it. Many professionals live in this realm and make those calls regularly, and if you are that person, know that you have my prayers, support, and respect. But since I've only been there one time, it still tears me apart to think about. I am forever grateful that I made that call.

It was day two of vacation Bible school, and we had four hundred kids and one hundred adults in the building. The day before, I had noticed a preteen girl who stood out a bit from the others. She constantly complained of being hungry and begged for extra food. She wasn't picked up until well after the normal time, so she hung out in the VBS headquarters area for a while. Her mom seemed stressed out. I did not think a whole lot of it.

But God got my attention on the second day when three different leaders approached me individually to express concern about her.

"Sarah, I don't want to make this a bigger deal than it should be, but I just want to mention that this girl in my class is super attached to my male youth helper. She won't leave his side and tries to hug or hang on him as much as possible."

"I don't want to cause any trouble, and it's probably nothing, but during art I noticed that she has some pretty bad bruises on her arms. Would you come take a look?"

"Hey, have you noticed that girl? She makes me worry. What do we know about her family?"

At the end of the day, I went to my supervisor and our executive director and unloaded all of this on them. I spouted all the evidence from the hunger to the bruises to the sexualized behavior, and at the end my executive director looked me in the eye and asked, "Did you just hear yourself? You literally just said, 'I suspect either abuse or neglect or both.' You have a responsibility now."

I was shocked. I only vaguely recalled uttering those words, but I knew they were true. Suddenly, this just got real. I arranged to have a conversation with the parents the following morning where I asked them about her hunger claims and offered any kind of help they might need. Both parents showed up for this meeting, and the father did all the talking, brushing aside any need for help with charm and confidence. "If anything, we give her too much to eat," he said.

From there, a colleague with professional experience as a school counselor came with me to call Child Protective Services. As I began relaying the family's personal information, the agent on the other end of the phone stopped typing—she already had them in her system, but they had lost touch. We arranged for CPS agents to come to the church the following day to meet with the family. After that meeting, I never saw or heard from them again.

I have no idea what happened. Were my suspicions correct? Did CPS take her away from her parents? Even though my curiosity just kills me, I try to remind myself that it's not my job to know that. My job is to make the call when I suspect harm, and that is all. Wherever this girl is now, God is with her.

Let's talk about something awful

I introduce every volunteer safety training with the words, "Listen, this is not going to be the most uplifting and life-giving conversation you and I are going to have about ministry to kids. This stuff is important, but you won't feel better afterward. I look forward to the more fun conversations we'll have after this one." That introduction applies to this whole chapter! Sorry not sorry.

With very little effort, you can find detailed information about what constitutes child abuse and what to do about it by going to sites such as the American Academy of Pediatrics *(aap.org)* or the Child Welfare Information Gateway *(childwelfare.gov)*. Bookmark these sites and return to them regularly for updated information. I will only provide a small piece of the overall puzzle here, with most of my information coming from child development textbooks and scholarly research studies.

. . . .

Abused children are all around us. We minister to them whether or not we are aware of it.

. . . .

Child abuse happens at every age and in every ethnicity and socioeconomic group, although calls to CPS are disproportionately high for minority groups. Children can experience abuse in any environment, from home to the church. One of the most common objections I hear to all the safety precautions we require is to look around at the volunteers in the children's ministry—they're mostly women, and all of them display such obvious moral character. What do we have to worry about?

In fact, ninety-three percent of sex offenders self-identify as religious, and twenty percent of abusers are female. Our churches are prime targets, and downplaying the importance of safety policies only endangers our kids. A statistic that you will hear over and over is that one in four girls and one in six boys will experience some form of abuse before turning eighteen. How many kids are in our church ministries? Do the sad math. Then repeat after me: Not. On. My. Watch.

Knowing the risk factors

A child who has experienced physical abuse may have bruises, especially in a pattern or on the face and head. Other markers to look for include bite marks, fractured ribs, and head injuries. Children with disabilities, military families (especially during deployment), children living with a nonrelated adult like a boyfriend or older sibling's friend, children in poverty, and children who have previously been reported to CPS all have a higher risk of abuse. Kids who have special needs or are withdrawn, loner types are more susceptible to abuse because the adult who takes advantage of them will count on these kids not to tell anyone or not to be believed if they do. Think through the kids in your ministry—which ones of them meet any of these criteria?

As leaders, we need to know how to spot not only the signs that a child has experienced abuse or neglect, but also the signs that a parent or volunteer may have abusive tendencies. Anytime we see an adult tease a child in a sexualized manner, take photos of a preteen in erotic poses, ask intrusive questions about a child's developing body, or invade a child's privacy while bathing, changing, or sleeping, we must act. Call the adult out on the behavior, document the interaction, and share it with your supervisor. This kind of behavior is grounds for removing that adult from contact with children in the church.

The same goes for an adult who plays roughly with a child or who uses physical force or angry words to discipline a child. Make it clear to your volunteers during training that only the gentlest discipline tactics, such as distracting the child or talking to the child's parents, are appropriate during ministry times. Listen to the language your team uses when talking to or about kids, and correct any shame or guilt-inducing phrases, such as, "Stop acting like a baby," or "You know better than that," or "You are such a pain." Good leaders correct kids' choices and guide kids' methods, but they have only uplifting and encouraging things to say about kids' personhood.

The vulnerability of preteens

Psychologists say that two important systems begin to develop in our brains during middle childhood (ages eight to ten). One of those systems incites risk-taking and prompts kids to start trying new things and seeking new sensory experiences. The purpose of this drive is to help them learn about their world and develop new abilities. This super fun system is balanced out by a calming, inhibiting system that helps control and monitor the risks we consider taking so that things don't get out of hand. The problem is that this second, protective system does not develop nearly as quickly as the first one does. This outpacing of these mental systems explains why preadolescents seem to make so many decisions without ever weighing the consequences.

Preteens experience the early stages of this phenomenon. Combine this evolving openness to risk with the trust that this age group still has for their world, especially for adults who are close to them, and we begin to understand how vulnerable they really are. Many of them haven't experienced real hurt yet. Most of them have only a limited understanding of sexual activity. They know just enough about the world and not enough about its dangers to be targets.

The good news is that while preteens still have much of the vulnerability of childhood, they also have the capacity to start to understand and articulate their experiences now, especially with our encouragement and willingness to listen. There is so much we can do to protect them!

Suicide Risk

Honestly, in the first draft of this chapter it did not occur to me to talk about suicide risk for preteens. However, when I sent it off to my own personal therapist to ask him to proofread it, his first question was whether I had considered talking about suicide. According to *Teen Suicide Risk* by King and Rogalski, suicide is the third leading cause of death for kids ages ten to fourteen. Girls are more likely to make a suicide attempt, but boys are more likely to be successful at it. By the time our kids reach age fourteen, suicide jumps to the number two spot in leading causes of death. What can we do during the preteen years to protect our kids later?

Studies show that teens usually give hints or outright tell a friend before they commit suicide. There are many risk factors, from poor sleep habits to mental illness and depression to abusive experiences, that contribute to a kid's risk for suicide. Parents and leaders who hear off-handed comments such as, "That won't be a problem for much longer," or who read suicidal thoughts in text messages, social media posts, or creative writing should take all these warning signs seriously.

And the best way to do that is to ask. In a matter-of-fact, informal, and nonjudgmental way, ask any preteen you are worried about if he or she has considered suicide. Some therapists recommend prefacing the question in a disarming way, such as:

"A lot of kids in your position think about suicide. Is that something you think about sometimes?"

"You are going through a lot of tough stuff right now, and I would understand if you had some thoughts about doing something drastic. Have you ever found yourself considering suicide?"

Just like talking about sex, we often hesitate to mention suicide because we don't want to put ideas into kids' heads that weren't there before. Let me reassure all of us on this point—the tragedy of a loving adult inadvertently planting suicidal ideas in a kid's head simply by addressing it doesn't happen. As Jen Hatmaker would say, that's not a thing. If a child is going to contemplate suicide, they'll do that without any impetus from us, and if a child is not suicidal, then talking about it will not cause harm. Talking about difficult issues only equips our kids to make better decisions when they confront them in the future. Everyone in a preteen's life is responsible for informal screening for suicide risk. It is a risk we can't afford to lose.

Sexting and pornography

If you want to see a preteen jaw drop, tell one of them how old you were when you got your first cell phone. (This probably only works for those of us born before 1990.) Better yet, show them what that first phone looked like. In 2016, the average age to receive a first cell phone was ten years old, and parents report that fifty percent of kids have a social media account before age twelve. And those are only the accounts that parents are aware of!

In 2010, the Kaiser Family Foundation found in a national survey that eight- to eighteen-year-olds spend on average seven hours and thirty-eight minutes a day using media for entertainment. Much of that time includes media multitasking, which means using multiple devices at the same time. By doing this, they cram a total of ten hours and forty-five minutes into those seven-and-a-half hours. Media in the form of TV, music, texting, and YouTube are their constant companions.

A friend of mine once told me that her third-grade daughter searched the Internet for "naked girls" because she was innocently curious to find out what she would look like after puberty. Another friend received a phone call from her son's school when he used his school-issued iPad to search "oral sex" because he heard the phrase on the bus and wondered what it was. Many kids stumble into pornography or receive an unsolicited sext message during their preteen years, and the impact of this exposure lasts a lifetime.

As ministry leaders, we have to keep in mind that even though these kids look so young, at least some of them carry experiences in their hearts that have aged them emotionally. Make sure they know that they can't shock you, that you are a safe place for them to share or ask questions about things they might have seen or heard. If you observe kids viewing porn or sending inappropriate texts in your ministry, talk to them and to their parents in a nonjudgmental, nonanxious way. Find a good, affordable pediatric therapist in your area, grab a stack of their business cards, and distribute them freely. Don't be afraid to deal with these issues when they arise, and know that if you're not seeing them during ministry time, that doesn't mean they're not happening all around these kids elsewhere.

Safe Sanctuaries

In The United Methodist Church, we refer to our whole posture toward protecting children, youth, and vulnerable adults as Safe Sanctuaries *(umc.org/umi/safe-sanctuaries)*. Every congregation is required to follow the denomination's requirements for safety and encouraged to build upon them. At the very least, every adult who works with children or youth must

- complete a background check (and renew every three years)
- complete Safe Sanctuaries training annually

- participate actively in the life of the church for at least six months prior to working with children, youth, or vulnerable adults

Some congregations also require volunteers to sign a covenant or share their motivations for serving within the ministry. The training that all volunteers receive covers procedural expectations, such as requiring two unrelated adults to be present at all times with children, managing bathroom breaks safely, observing and reporting abuse, keeping attendance records, and checking kids in and out of events safely. Depending on the audience, the trainings I run typically last thirty minutes or so. It's a small investment for producing volunteers I can trust, and training them this way protects the adults just as much as the kids.

Preteens present a few nuances in training, and if I am talking to a group of leaders who work specifically with this group, I give extra attention to the areas of travel, games, private conversations, and physical contact.

Travel

Preteens are the first age group that is likely to travel without their parents for church retreats, camps, or mission projects. Always keep in mind that their risk-taking impulses will not be checked by anyone but you, which requires your constant vigilance. Every time I have taken a group of preteens to play laser tag, I leave with an anxiety hangover. I now know it is all but impossible to keep track of thirty preteens in a dark building where everyone wears the same neon vests.

One of the major tenets of Safe Sanctuaries is head counts—always know who is in your group and count vigilantly to ensure no one is missing. But as soon as you scatter a cluster of preteens in an arcade or amusement park or campground, head counts become a shared responsibility. When traveling, endeavor to assign a one-to-five ratio of adults to kids. And by "assign," I mean literally partner up one adult with five specific kids to keep track of. That number is chosen for practical reasons, just because it is hard for me to imagine keeping track of more than five preteens for a field trip. But if you have a limited number of volunteers, make the groups as small as you can.

Another warning about travel—seat belts! It doesn't occur to most second-graders to try to evade the seat belt rule while on a church bus, but I have entered verbal negotiations with preteens over this issue. Don't trust them to click it. Make sure they do.

These issues are just two examples of the importance of the number one travel rule: don't ever go by yourself. Always have at least one other unrelated adult at your side who is fully invested in caring for the kids with you. That means that the guy who drives the bus you rented does not count. Learn from my mistakes on this one—it was no fun to leave a bus full of third- through fifth-grade boys unattended in their seats on the side of the highway while I exited to talk to the man whose bumper I had just tapped. Mercifully, I was not fired and no one was hurt, but that was a terrible way to learn my lesson.

Games

Finally!—a group of kids that can handle dodgeball or a game of H.O.R.S.E. If you are so lucky as to have recruited a young person to help lead preteens, you might find that this robust individual's spiritual gift appears to consist of pegging kids in the knees with power throws. Never forget that preteens are still kids, most of whom haven't started their growth spurt yet. Help your volunteers prioritize the safety of kids above winning a game designed for people half their age. Observe both leaders and kids closely during games, and step in anytime you sense somebody could get hurt.

Another pitfall of group games for preteens is the ever-present phenomenon of cliques. Whenever possible, assign teams randomly rather than letting preteens choose. If one of your church kids brought a friend from outside the church, keep those two together at all times. Other than that, split people up as often as possible. There is no harm in forcing the kids in your church to get to know each other better.

Those sweet, quiet kids present another consideration. While we always have to keep our eyes out for wallflowers, it becomes even more imperative during games. Aloneness can be amplified during group recreation. Often, being quiet is a comfortable place to stay during group discussions or when listening to a Bible study, but when you shift to a group game, that shy personality can start to feel very left out. I do not force kids to participate in games if they don't want to—you never know who just started her period and isn't comfortable moving around or who is too embarrassed to explain about his ingrown toenail that makes running painful, so don't push that. Design your game times to be inclusive of the girl whose growth spurt kicked in early, the boy who hasn't grown an inch since he was eight, and everyone in between.

Private conversations

Having instructed my volunteers to make themselves available to preteens who might want to confide in them or ask difficult questions, I then need to show them how to receive these conversations safely. Our policy is that two adults are always present with kids during ministry times. If a preteen asks a trusted adult to talk privately, I want to respect that need for privacy while also protecting the adult from any possible reproach and the kid from any secret actions.

If a preteen asks you to talk privately, first ask if they're comfortable talking to you plus one other trained leader. If not, then simply ask another adult to "stand watch." Tell the second adult that the preteen has asked to speak privately, and you need the other adult both to be aware that the conversation is taking place and to stay within view throughout it. This can mean one adult stands on the other side of a window and observes without being able to hear the conversation inside the room. It can also mean you sit in the hallway to talk with the preteen while the person on watch sits a few yards away, able to see but not hear. In short, make sure that someone else always has your back and can give a good and full report of everything that transpired during the conversation.

Physical contact

The number one rule of physical contact with preteens: respect their space and privacy. The phrase I leave with all my volunteers is to be "above reproach." Is there a place for hugs with preteens? Yes, there is. But think of them like you would your boss—you may really like them and feel a bond, but there is a level of respect that supersedes all other impulses.

If you ever find yourself or observe another adult getting too physical with a preteen, call it out immediately. There is no room for hesitation. My go-to physical interaction with kids is a high five. They can choose whether or not to take you up on the invitation, and if they do, they are in control of the velocity and impact of the connection.

"I'll only hug kids if they initiate it" is not good enough. These kids are experiencing hormonal shifts for the first time, and the likelihood that one of them will have a crush on you at any one point is high and normal. Being the adults makes us the caretakers. I accept most hugs when they are offered, but if you find that you've hugged a preteen three times in the same day, it's probably time to step back the next time you're approached with outstretched arms and say, "How about a high five?" or "Do you know who super needs a hug today? Your pal Sadie."

Just to give the dead horse one more thwack, I say again: the first time that you or another adult makes physical contact with a preteen in anger or roughness is the last time.

Observing and reporting

Research has shown that some kids are masterminds of hiding their emotions, which means it is rare for a preteen to admit to an adult whenever things are bad at home. As someone on the front lines of preteen ministry, you are one of the best possible people to pick up on warning signs of abuse. Engage your Spidey-sense, and don't be afraid to be the one who is always going to your supervisor with suspicions. I know this sounds paranoid and subjective, but tune in to your instincts. This is not a fear we can repress, and when it comes to kids' safety, there is no such thing as hoping for the best. Speak up.

If you do detect any warning sign, including sudden withdrawal of a kid who was formerly engaged in the group, an overbearing and overprotective parent who speaks defensively of his or her home life, a preteen who uses sexual language that seems too knowledgeable for his or her age, or physical injury, report it. As good citizens, we have a responsibility to call the Department of Social Services for any suspicion of abuse or neglect. Just make sure you always clue in your supervisor or a church staff person before doing so. Let that person walk alongside you. If your supervisor happens to be the parent of the child, this is the one instance in which it is appropriate to skip a level of the organizational chart and talk to that person's supervisor.

It is not our job to prove or demonstrate that something bad has happened. It is our job to share our concerns with the appropriate people. As a counterpart to looking for harm, here are a few factors that tend to protect children and prevent abuse in the home:

- Parental resilience—a parent's own ability to cope with stress
- Parental knowledge of child development and parenting skills
- Concrete support in times of need
- Social connections
- A child's ability to form positive relationships

Do you see it? These research-based, proven measures of child protection are all things that the church can provide.

. . . .

How many children could be safer if they and their parents could say they found support, connection, and education from the church?

. . . .

Ministry starts with safety and builds from there. Next, we get to explore a few powerful areas that almost all preteens are just beginning to navigate.

Online access

My preteen ministry has a strict "no cell phone" policy, and I inform parents of this prior to any retreat or class. Cell phones that pose distractions are confiscated and returned to kids at the end of our time together. Any kids who worry about getting in touch with a parent can use my phone to make a call or text whenever needed. Turns out, that need seldom arises.

Be careful which photos you and your leaders post to social media. The best practice is to only post photos taken during ministry time through your church's official social media accounts—and only for kids whose parents have signed a photo release. Any photos posted by parents or leaders need to be taken down. Families should be able to expect that their kids will not be visible on the Internet without their permission.

Rather than bemoan the rise of technology use, we should celebrate the good that it offers while preventing it from interfering with God's work in our ministry times. Kids will tune us out the moment we begin to disrespect their primary communication, courtship, and connection tool. Instead, let's show them how to practice spiritual disciplines through their media use. During your ministry times, practice unplugging and being quiet, two states they don't experience all that often. But also, show them the apps you use for daily Bible reading and devotions. Have them crowdsource their favorite worship music, and encourage them to create their own playlist for meditation, reflection, or personal worship at home. Teach Scriptures that speak to discernment and moderation.

At the end of this chapter, there are several resources that can be used to address some of the dangers of social media and over-sharing that preteens are susceptible to. Check them out if those are areas for which the parents of your preteens need help. We can't and probably shouldn't remove kids' access to technology, but we do have to recognize the impact of the marketing campaigns to which it exposes them.

Advertising to preteens

This age group is heavily targeted by consumer marketers, and they are absolutely buying in. Preteens are an advertiser's dream audience because they show little inhibition about sharing personal information online, which means they fill in those little pop-up boxes that ask for names and e-mails without a second thought. They also tend to be big spenders. Children in the US between the ages of eight to thirteen spend about forty billion on their own annually and influence countless more dollars of their parents' spending.

Because these preteen years are so devoted to identity development, products that promise popularity, high self-esteem, a concrete gender identity, and social success are almost irresistible. Marketers also believe that if they can get a preteen's loyalty to their brand, they'll have that loyalty for life.

One danger here is something called "age compression," pushing adult habits on younger and younger kids. Or, as the head of marketing at Disney Radio puts it, K-GOY: Kids Getting Older Younger.

In their efforts to take preteens' money, advertisers teach them a dangerous and false worldview: sexy is cool, any attention is good attention, outward appearance is the most important thing, responsibility is uncool, and life should only be fun. With every Bible study we prepare and every group activity we lead, we should remember that our preteens hear a very different message from almost every other source in their worlds. One of the best counterbalances I have found to the power of preteen marketing is to offer a faith-based, comprehensive sex education ministry.

Faith & sexuality

I have saved the best for last! If you have never experienced the pure joy of teaching preteens to see themselves as God's creations, I hope you will find a way to introduce this element to your ministry soon. Learning about the body, intimacy, sex, and reproduction is a rite of passage that too many of us remember with regret or even pain.

One of the best gifts we can give to our preteens is a fearless identity as God's creation, complete with sexual feelings.

If the idea of gathering all the preteens into your church and talking to them about sex makes you hyperventilate, grab a brown paper bag and stick with me. There really is something special about coming to church to learn how God's love and your body work together. We are in the unique position of ministering to the whole family—we can empower parents and educate kids in a way that is norm-setting, since everyone is in it together. When an anxious preteen (and his or her even more anxious parent) looks around the room and realizes that he or she is not alone, this topic that first seemed so untouchable becomes simpler.

As always, the best place for kids to understand sexuality is in a home where no topic is off limits and parents listen and give honest, loving answers. The church cannot instill a lifelong sexual ethic in kids through one long weekend event. However, putting an event on the church calendar doesn't just offer a one-time conversation; it communicates to your people that the church considers sexuality to be an important and beautiful part of God's creation and that we're open to talking about it. It encourages families to go ahead and schedule some of those conversations with their kids, rather than waiting for it to come up on its own.

How does church sex education keep preteens safe?

So many of the dangers to preteens and adolescents stem from sex. If we leave preteens in the dark about sex and all the emotional, developmental, and spiritual effects of it, they will see no other option than to follow the lead of friends and advertisers. The consequences of sexual sharing or shaming can be devastating.

In your church, you minister to kids who are noticing same-sex attraction for perhaps the first time. You minister to kids from households where sex is a dirty word and having a crush on a friend is punishable by relentless teasing. You minister to kids whose parents laugh about buying them condoms someday and love reliving the tales of their happy and promiscuous glory days of college. You minister to kids whose only knowledge of sex comes in the form of abuse and manipulation. And all these kids are subject to lies from Hollywood and pressure from peers to meet an unattainable ideal of sexy.

Sex is a beautiful, loving gift from God, and it is sacred. It can be a gift or a weapon. One of the best ways we can protect the kids in our church from harm is to position ourselves as a safe place to share, ask questions, and learn about sex.

Why preteens?

In my experience, the best time to start a church conversation about sexuality is in fifth grade. While some fourth-graders (especially girls) are ready and eager and asking questions, most of the kids in fourth grade (especially boys) are not. For parents of fourth-graders who insist that their child is ready (and they are probably right), send home the reading materials and encourage them to study and talk at home, but I suggest waiting to include them in a formal church event until they can experience it along with their peers.

In fifth grade, most kids are developmentally and cognitively ready to accept information about puberty, intimacy, intercourse, and difficult topics like abortion, abstinence, birth control, and rape. The best moment to share comprehensive information about sex is when they are interested in learning and still surprised by what they learn. We want to be the first ones to share with them. The kids in your preteen ministry want to ask these questions, and they deserve to hear honest and loving answers.

How faith and sexuality events work

There are as many methods for faith and sexuality events as there are churches, and you will want to design yours around the size and demographics of your congregation. I have served in a 3,000-member church and a 150-member church, and the following ideas have guided me in both places.

Age—We offer completely different events for fifth-graders and sixth-graders. The program for fifth-graders is very grounded in learning anatomy and physiology. There is a significant focus on learning vocabulary and normalizing the use of accurate language to describe sexuality. We define a lot of terms and introduce a balanced approach to difficult subjects. We do not prescribe what they should believe about controversial subjects such as sexual orientation or birth control, but we do preach the message of abstinence until marriage within the context of comprehensive knowledge of sex.

For sixth-graders, that basic material is old news. In middle schools, oral sex is often considered a rite of passage or a way to experiment that is not "really sex." They are ready to start exploring the relational and situational side of sex. They are starting to collect sexual experiences, whether that means receiving a sexual solicitation from a peer, sexting, public shaming, or supporting a pregnant friend. They need a place full of trusted adults where they can feel safe sharing about their worries or experiences and receiving guidance. The material we cover with them builds upon what they learned in fifth grade.

While I am convinced that by fifth grade kids are ready to learn about sexuality, I do not want to imply that only the church can teach it. Parents who want that responsibility for themselves should be resourced and encouraged! Whether a child participates in a church event or learns at home, all that matters is that this milestone should be crossed during these preteen years with an intentional guide.

Event Structure—This is different for almost every church. Some pack as much as they can into one Sunday afternoon session, while others create a six-week curriculum to teach on Sunday mornings. My preference for fifth-graders is for an intense, high-commitment weekend designed to set a foundation.

For sixth-graders, the exposure to social sexuality evolves over the course of the whole school year. Assuming that they all have the resources at home to reference the basics, they need a regular invitation to share their concerns and learn how to navigate the situations they face. Any emphasis on faith and sexuality for this age group should span at least several weeks. If possible, the best approach is an ongoing small group with a regular emphasis on sexuality as part of our spirituality. A small group that is built upon accountability and acceptance is the best support we can give them.

Parent Component—We require at least one parent from each household to participate in a gathering beforehand. This parent meeting provides the chance to present ourselves as their partners. We recognize that they are the primary sex educators for their kids, but we want to provide a safe place for their family to ask questions or seek support. We remind them that we can only invest a small amount of time in their kids, but they can participate in this conversation over time. We also meet with fifth-grade parents after the retreat to reassure them that everything went well, hear what their kids have been saying, and reinforce the need for ongoing conversation in their households. We use this time to inform them of all the topics we will cover with their kids, to give them materials to use at home, and to allow them to ask questions.

Volunteers—The only qualification I look for when seeking volunteers for this ministry (other than the standard requirements for every supervisory adult) is a willingness to encounter awkward conversations with preteens. The first people I usually approach are pediatricians, counselors, and other medical professionals, but that's not necessary. The only adults who are not encouraged to lead in this area are parents of participating kids. They have an at-home role and generally need to be ministered to through this process as much as their kids do. This volunteer team participates in a special training meeting prior to any parent meetings, and team members are expected to attend all parent meetings if they can.

Internal or Invitational—Some churches keep their faith and sexuality event internal in order to preserve intimacy among the preteens who will continue to grow up together in the church. It is also important to keep the ratio of participants to adult leaders low. However, my preference is to open these kinds of events to friends outside the church. Christian parents aren't the only ones who struggle to cover this topic with their kids, and these events can surprisingly appeal to a wide range of people who otherwise wouldn't enter your church. Who would have thought that teaching about sex could be so evangelistic?

Another fantastic option is for churches to join up to offer the retreat for fifth-graders. Talk to other pastors or preteen leaders in your town to see if they would be interested in pooling budgets and volunteers to offer this training in your community.

Final thoughts

It is crazy that a depressing topic like safety can be inspired by such deep love, but it is true. I hope that as you waded through all of this, you identified some practices that can make your ministry safer and also felt the swell of love and protection for this age group.

One of my favorite Old Testament stories is from Exodus 17, the Battle of Rephidim. Overlooking our mutual discomfort about the violent fighting that takes place in this story, I love the imagery of Moses' role. He sat with two helpers up on a hillside to observe the battle, and he realized that when he raised his hands, his people advanced, but when he let his hands down, his people lost ground. For a whole day, with the help of two friends, Moses kept his hands in the air, and Israel won.

Our role is to keep our hands in the air too. While our kids face adversaries in their friendships, purchases, advertising, homes, friend's houses, and phones every day, in the church we hold our hands high and declare our space to be safe. We do the work of preparing our leaders, holding adults accountable for their actions with children and educating our church's kids to navigate the perilous pathway of puberty and peer pressure. We can't guard them every minute of every day—not even their parents can—but we must make church as safe a place as they'll ever enter.

CHAPTER 5

INCLUDE

> But as it is, there are many parts but one body. So the eye can't say to the hand, "I don't need you," or in turn, the head can't say to the feet, "I don't need you." Instead, the parts of the body that people think are the weakest are the most necessary. The parts of our body that we think are less honorable are the ones we honor the most. The private parts of our body that aren't presentable are the ones that are given the most dignity. The parts of our body that are presentable don't need this.

> But God has put the body together, giving greater honor to the part with less honor so that there won't be division in the body and so the parts might have mutual concern for each other. If one part suffers, all the parts suffer with it; if one part gets the glory, all the parts celebrate with it.

> You are the body of Christ and parts of each other.
> (*1 Corinthians 12:20-27*)

Every one of us has special needs—some are just more visible than others. In the church, Paul says we are all part of one Body and should have mutual concern for each other. In keeping with Jesus' teaching that the last should be first and the first last, the parts of the Body we wouldn't naturally elevate have greater honor in God's kingdom.

This is the most intimidating chapter in the book for me to write. Dedicating one chapter of a short book to the topic of inclusion in preteen ministry is admittedly a little crazy. There is no way I can do this topic justice, both because my own experience in this area is of the DIY, homespun variety, and because this topic warrants so much more discussion. Still, there is no way I can leave it out either. A large number of the preteens we love and care for have disabilities, both hidden and visible.

. . . .

This is not about catering to a small subset of preteens. This is a philosophy of inclusion and care that should guide our whole ministry.

. . . .

I'm going to put my number-one secret of inclusive ministry right here at the beginning, so you don't even have to read through the whole chapter to get it. Here you go: we should design ministry around the needs of the outliers. We should start by considering the needs of kids who don't fit the mold. Has everyone seen that object lesson in which someone tries to fit a set of seashells and a vial of sand into a jar? If you pour the sand in first, there isn't room for the shells, but if you fit each shell in first, the sand can fill in the cracks and everything fits. I really hope you've seen this done before because otherwise my description is going to flop.

In this scenario, kids with sensitivities, disabilities, special needs, ticks, behavior problems, or other difficulties are the seashells, each one beautiful and unique. If we plan for their needs first, the rest of the group—the sand—will flow into place easily. Start with special needs in mind when you choose paint colors and decide on bathroom policies and select curriculum. Train volunteers to speak lovingly into the lives of the kids who are least comfortable in the setting. The sound level of the mixing board and the introduction and closing procedures for small-group times should all be based on the needs of kids with anxiety, ADHD, autism, Down Syndrome, mood disorders, ambulatory needs, and speech and hearing disorders. In meeting the needs of preteens with disabilities, you will by default meet the needs of the whole group.

I hope I can provide a few strategies here to help you include every kind of preteen in your ministry.

Serving preteens with disabilities

How do we define disabilities? To look at my family, no one would think that we have any special needs. However, those closest to me know that one of my sons cannot handle bright light and often takes an hour to adjust to normal lighting when he first wakes up, and my other son struggles with any loud noises, including the drumbeat of our church's worship band. Do these count?

To steal a phrase from the Nathaniel's Hope website (dedicated to providing resources for respite care, which I'll get to later), special needs include "kids with any physical, cognitive, medical or hidden disability, chronic or life-threatening illness or those who are medically fragile." At times, I have expanded this definition to include severe allergies, which can often limit a child's ability to participate in church activities. Here is the main thing: if a child could benefit from an accommodation we can provide, then we should provide it. If a parent asks for help or conveys a worry about her child, we should take her seriously.

Those of us without serious disabilities can easily begin thinking we are more objective than the families who are in the trenches of a child's disability. We see a parent allow his child to play on an iPad throughout worship and think he is coddling him or we notice a family with a special needs child has missed a lot of church lately and wish they would make more of an effort. But the truth is, unless we live their lives, we have no idea about the struggles they deal with daily. Our role is not to determine what is best; it is to listen, support, and provide any accommodations we can.

Remember that chapter on calling?

I have found that the most effective method for including kids with special needs is to point out their own specific talents and abilities, and put those to work while at church. Just about every preteen I've ever met likes having a job to do, and this is especially true for those who may feel more uncomfortable than most in social situations. Having a disability is just one piece of a preteen's life experience. When we put the emphasis of our ministry time on helping preteens to discern their callings, we create a level playing field where everyone is treasured and it's okay to be different.

At a retreat one year, I became concerned for one of the girls who did not seem to have the confidence or social skills to enter a friend circle. She wore thick glasses and had unruly hair, and the rest of the kids did not know how to include her. As a small step toward helping her to a place of belonging, we gave her a job. She took over the snack table— setting it up, replenishing snacks from the fridge, throwing away used cartons. She was the behind-the-scenes organizer, able to bless others by offering food.

In my Sunday morning ministry time, I have a beloved sidekick that helps me out every time we're together. His name is Nick, and Nick has some impulsivity and attention issues that make it impossible to sit quietly for thirty minutes and only speak after raising his hand. So, Nick is my personal assistant. If I'm telling a story, Nick is standing next to me, holding the poster for the other kids to see the picture. When it's time to circle up and share prayer requests, Nick retrieves the electric candle that we pass and hands it to each kid who wants to share. When we transition back to the sanctuary to take Communion, Nick goes with me to pick up preschoolers and bring them to their parents, because transition times are hard for him and he'd rather help out.

The point is, let's not forget that no matter what a child's abilities are, they are all called to do God's work just like we are. By focusing on their identity as God's children and the work God has for them to do, we can create an inclusive ministry that goes beyond just a warm welcome and becomes a place of belonging and respect.

Beyond this general strategy of helping preteens with disabilities to work out their calling stories, I want to share a few other ideas that have worked well for me in the past. The following are just a few suggestions based on my experiences.

Creating an inclusive ministry

First, let's agree that it doesn't take a mega-church or a finely tuned disability ministry to include preteens with special needs. Churches of every size and skill level can welcome almost anyone if they simply adopt the approach of "one person at a time." Sometimes we get caught up in thinking we should build it first and then they will come. That philosophy may work for baseball stadiums, but it's an ineffective beginning for an inclusive preteen ministry.

The goal is that from senior pastor to parishioner to kid in the pew, we all agree that we will love every person, one at a time. Again, every one of us has special needs, whether a psychologist has helped us label them or not. None of us wants to have our participation decided for us based upon a cursory glance. We want to be seen for who we really are and to share our own stories.

There are no cookie cutters for ministry. To be truly inclusive, commit to being both creative and honest. Build your ministry around your people, not around a curriculum, and certainly not what the church down the street is doing. Send the message to every person who enters your door that you want to know and care for that person individually.

I need to recognize here that while I have emphasized the fact that each of us has some version of special needs, I also should clarify that those with certain disabilities work twice as hard to achieve the same recognition and level of participation as an able-bodied or neurotypical peer. The trick is to recognize the universal need for acceptance, while at the same time committing to find unique ways to include those with disabilities.

I have found that all most parents are looking for when they bring their kids to a new church is a group of people who will truly care for their child. This hope is illustrated beautifully in an article written by Sandra Peoples, mom to a son with special needs, who wrote about her experience trying a new church: "There's really just two things I want from the church we attend: I want them to keep James safe and I want them to love him." She went on to quote the greeting she received from the pastor within five minutes of entering a church: "We're so glad you're here and we don't want you to worry about James at all."

If all we do is greet every new family like this with the assurance that we have a safe place prepared for their kids or will create a safe place based on their needs, we have succeeded. Our message to every preteen is, "There is a place for you here." Sometimes we follow that up with a let's-figure-this-out-now attitude, but that's okay. Parents of preteens who don't fit into any mold tell me they are accustomed to being denied or rejected. An acknowledgment that you want to do the work to make your church a safe and fun environment for their child is like water on dry ground.

. . . .

Start becoming inclusive by examining the message you send to each preteen who comes through the door.

. . . .

Are they greeted by a live person? Does that person know where to direct them if they have needs or questions? Does that person smile? Do they encounter a loud, crowded room right off the bat?

A cheerful greeter who can guide each arrival to the appropriate destination is key. In my church, our hospitality team has been coached to walk any newcomer families to the children's area and walk them through the check-in process. If a family member has a special need, a member of the team will quickly seek out myself or our senior pastor to give us a heads-up, and then one or both of us will greet the family to let them know how glad we are they came and to ask how we can best care for their child.

Every person with disabilities is different, so it's important to creatively adapt your ministry based on the preteens who walk through your doors. That said, there are some broad procedures you can implement which will affect your whole ministry but are specifically designed to help kids with special needs.

Make a welcoming space

Those of us who look forward to the social time before worship or the noisy cheering that precedes a youth-ministry large-group session should keep in mind that others with social anxiety or sensory issues may dread these same things. Bright lights and loud music can feel painful to someone who is easily overstimulated. Many families find pageantry and a party atmosphere attractive, and I think our hope with these kinds of environments is that kids will find church fun. There may be a place for blaring speakers in ministry with kids, but we need to keep in mind that they are not welcoming to some kids. Whenever possible, create a quiet entry point that can at least allow a slower transition into a possibly overwhelming environment.

Another basic rule is muted decor in your children and youth areas. Kids respond to their surroundings, and kids with sensory processing disorders can feel overwhelmed easily. When possible, choose pastel or gray paint and carpet colors, and don't overdo the posters and knickknacks on your walls. Basically, look at any preschool classroom in America and do the opposite of that. Now you can ask anyone who knows me, and they'll tell you that I have no place giving decorating advice. My idea of window treatments begins and ends with the blinds that came with my house. But after talking to occupational therapists and observing the decor in most counselors' offices, I'm convinced that we should keep our ministry spaces underwhelming.

Of course, these accessibility suggestions are in addition to the public accommodations provisions of the Americans with Disabilities Act. While churches are not legally required to provide wheelchair access, accessible bathrooms, and so forth, voluntarily complying sends a message of inclusivity. If your church is large, make sure your hospitality team knows how to direct someone from the front entrance to the children's area using the elevator or ramps.

Start the conversation

Every youth and children's ministry should require a form that asks for allergy, health, and personal information from any kid who has attended three times or more. Some families with kids who have a disability will contact you ahead of time to request accommodations, and in that case you can provide this form ahead of their first visit. Otherwise, there should be a system in place to monitor attendance records and invite families to complete a form. Once a parent turns in this form, start a conversation with that parent about how best to ensure a good, safe experience for their child.

The next step is to prepare the volunteers who will work with that child. Best practice is to summarize the relevant information you have gleaned from the health form and conversations with the parent into a separate document. Make sure the parents have a chance to approve the document, and then hand it to the volunteers. Sometimes, parents will have already prepared such a document for other caregivers, which you can adapt as necessary. If there are emergency medical instructions for a child, store those instructions in a safe spot in the room where the child will spend most of his church time.

Creatively accommodate

Serving families of preteens with disabilities requires flexibility and a willingness to adapt our rules and boundaries. Again, here's the big secret: we minister to kids one at a time. For example, a child with a disability might be a better fit for a small group that is either slightly younger or slightly older than that child's physical age. I usually keep my age restrictions for preteens pretty strict, but would I consider allowing a ten-year-old child to attend kindergarten through third-grade kids' worship if the parents thought that was a better fit? Absolutely.

If I see a child walking through a church hallway between services with gigantic headphones on, my first reaction is often to think, "Antisocial much?" In my less judgmental moments, which admittedly are scarce, I can concede that perhaps the stress of transition times and noise of gathering spaces constitute sensory overload, and for this child the choice is either wear headphones or sit in the car. Headphones are better. Consider purchasing some earplugs or noise-canceling headphones and making them easily available for preteens to pick up.

In general, we will find it simpler to include kids with physical disabilities than kids with social or emotional disabilities. When a challenge is immediately visible, it is easier to address. It is more socially acceptable to see a child in a wheelchair and immediately offer assistance than to say anything to a parent whose child appears physically normal, but behaves atypically. I honestly congratulate any children's ministry that extends accommodations to a preteen with a physical disability—that is step one. Next, we need to learn how to recognize and support social and emotional disabilities as well.

Including preteens with less overt disabilities sometimes means understanding socially inappropriate behavior as part of a preteen's struggle to read social and emotional cues. Once, a young guy who has autism burst into his Sunday-morning small-group room and exclaimed, "What the f*** is going on in here?" I can't help but laugh when I think of the stunned silence and petrified faces of all the other kids in his class. Thank the Lord, his teacher was a cool operator, and without missing a beat, she invited him to sit down and then led the whole class in a discussion about language and what it means. Instead of flipping out or openly chastising this kid whom she clearly adored, she helped him to learn a more appropriate social script while also explaining his behavior to the rest of the group.

Keep Consistent Routines

For people with anxiety or other disabilities that make social interaction stressful, every interaction at church is hard. One way that anxiety manifests in preteens is in difficulties separating from parents—we tend to think of separation anxiety as a little kid problem, but it can rear up in the preteen years as well and often precedes anxiety problems in the future. It is not unusual to find that a preteen prefers going with his parents to their class or has a meltdown at the drop-off door.

We cannot step into the parents' role and decide how to deal with these kinds of fears. The best aid we can offer is to keep the weekly routine as consistent as possible and encourage the family to keep trying. Start small groups at the start time and end at the appropriate end time, every week. Follow a similar structure every week—try not to swap large-/small-group times around without warning or spend one Sunday a month going on a field trip. If a preteen learns what to expect from your ministry time, she will have a much easier time battling the "what if" anxieties that try to take over every week.

Preteens are learning to operate in a socially-driven world, some for the first time. But disability can make social interactions painfully hard. Developmentally, preteens all experience a surge in desiring to fit in and please their internal audience. For kids with social or emotional disabilities, those internal audiences can be crueler than most. We should try to limit the surprises that a preteen will encounter during normal ministry times as much as possible, giving our kids the ability to anticipate what's next and step into it confidently.

Prepare for participation

That said, it's clearly not possible to do the exact same thing every week without deviation. Retreats, concerts, lock-ins, field trips, guest speakers, summer camp, and a plethora of other special events provide quality ministry time for our preteens, and we can't shy away from these opportunities. We can, however, help our preteens anticipate them and navigate them with as little stress as possible.

When planning a special event, provide details ahead of time to all families. And when I say "details," I mean start time, end time, location, photos, names of leaders, leader bios, topical outline of what will be discussed, list of physical activities, directions to and from the location, contact information for leaders and other parents . . . and anything else you can think of. Help the parents of anxious preteens paint a clear picture to their kids of what to expect. Spell it all out. Keep no secrets.

Another way to prepare kids for participation is to provide them with appropriate verbal scripts. Most kids with autism, anxiety, ADHD, and many other social/emotional disabilities have typical intelligence for their age. Their capacity for participation and understanding is on par with everyone else in the group and potentially much higher. The problem arises in preteen ministry when we start to focus heavily on small-group interactions—as we should—without recognizing that these social situations are the most difficult territory for some preteens to navigate. One great way to help all kids feel more comfortable is to provide scripts for them to use. It could sound like this:

"Okay, people, I'm going to read from the Bible here in a minute, and I want everyone to listen closely. When I'm done, I'm going to say, 'This is the Word of God for the people of God,' and you're all going to respond, 'Thanks be to God.' Let's practice that a couple of times first."

"Friends, this morning we're talking about courage—what it means, examples we've seen or read about courage, and what God has to say about courage. Everyone will have a chance to share if you want. If you don't want to share, I want you to say, 'No, thanks,' when I ask you a question, okay? And after anyone shares, I want everyone else to say in unison, 'Thanks for sharing,' even if you disagree or don't like what the person said. Understood? Let's practice that."

"Patrick, I love that you have such a great point to make, but you interrupted Andrew to make it. I need everyone to wait your turn to speak. If you have something that you really, really want to say, I want you to keep listening, and then raise your hand as soon as the first person is done speaking. I want to hear all of your genius ideas, so please be patient—we'll get to you, I promise!"

Giving your preteens clear and loving guidance for the way you expect preteens to interact is a huge favor to them.

Listen and trust

When a parent asks to talk to you and shares about difficulties they're having with their son or daughter or when a preteen tells you that the music hurts her ears or when you find a kid sitting in the hall with his head in his lap, crying because someone was mean to him—listen. Listen to the exact words that the person is telling you, and trust that they are speaking honestly from their experience. Validate their feelings with responses like, "That is so hard," or "I hear what you are saying, and I am so sorry you have to deal with this."

Follow those responses up with, "I will help you figure this out." We need some open-mindedness when it comes to finding a safe and comfortable place of belonging for some kids. When a preteen who had behaved typically all his life suddenly started showing out-of-control separation anxiety from parents and a complete refusal to participate in his small group, he became our Sunday School Helper. I put him to work, sorting nametags and putting away snacks and organizing the gym equipment. He was always supervised by two unrelated adults, and his parents signed off on the arrangement. It was not ideal, but it was a place of belonging that did not stress him out and allowed his parents to participate in their group, so it worked.

When a couple of kids have complained that the music at vacation Bible school is too loud for them, we let them skip that rotation and hang out in the VBS headquarters area where several adults dote on them and give them extra snacks for those twenty minutes. Are these kids playing the system? Possibly, but I don't really care. My mission is for kids to know that they are loved and are safe, and if I can accomplish that, I'm content.

Teach inclusivity to all kids

For a preteen who is utterly preoccupied with fitting in and following every social cue, including someone who stands out as different can go completely against nature. In fact, I would attest that it is just as important to help all our preteens develop empathy as it is to provide accommodations to those who need them. The first step to create an inclusive environment is to educate the preteens who are already there, keeping in mind that some of them may have hidden disabilities or needs that you're not even aware of.

Most of us do not learn how to exit our comfortable coexistence with those around us in order to be vulnerable or risk rejection, even as adults. Imagine if we had affirming and supportive experiences during our preteen years in which we both took initiative to connect with friends who were different from us and also received those kinds of connections from others. Nothing is scarier for a preteen than putting popularity on the line, but teaching inclusion during these malleable years can make a lifetime impact on these kids' perception of friendship and community.

Model inclusion by making overt efforts to greet and talk to every kid in your group—no one should ever leave the building without having heard his or her name from a loving leader multiple times. Talk about inclusion by sharing expectations with your group about how they'll treat one another and any newcomers, and get specific. If you feel you have established a safe place for kids to share, open the floor for them to talk about what inclusion (or exclusion) looks like to them. Respond to every sharing with, "Thank you for telling us that. You are God's child, and we love you."

Beyond that general approach, one specific best practice for creating a climate of belonging is the buddy talk. This is an intentional conversation with a group of peers, usually led by the ministry leader but sometimes by a child's parent, when you can educate the kids on loving ways to include a particular friend and help them understand and feel affection for her. For example,

- If a friend experiences seizures, explain to the group in age-appropriate terms what a seizure is and how to notice if their friend seizes. Assure them that the adults in the room will take care of everything if a seizure happens and they don't need to worry about what to do, other than telling an adult if they have a concern.

- If a preteen friend has an intellectual disability, work with parents to identify the group activities that might be uncomfortable for her, such as reading from the Bible. Identify ways the group can help, such as making sure she has a reading buddy when it's time to pull out Scripture. Then share with the group that this friend would appreciate having a reading buddy. Ask the group members to agree to step in to help their friend without waiting to be asked by an adult every time the group reads Scripture.

- If a friend has autism, invite three other specific friends to be that child's buddies. Talk to the parents of these buddies to let them know you'd like their child to participate in this leadership opportunity. Sit down with these buddies to share their job description, which is basically to be intentional about being a good friend. Point out the kinds of social cues the preteen with autism may struggle with, difficult triggers, and helpful redirection phrases. Once the buddies are prepared, introduce them to their new friend and tell the preteen with autism that he can count on these three friends to lend a helping hand anytime.

Offer respite care

Often the first step toward recruiting volunteers who are comfortable around kids with disabilities, as well as attracting families affected by disability to your church, is to offer respite care. Usually, this looks like opening your church one evening a month or a quarter to provide three or four hours of safe, quality childcare for kids with disabilities. In the Suggested Resources section at the end of this chapter, you'll find a couple of organizations specifically aimed at helping churches offer quality respite care. This is the most frequently requested ministry I have encountered from families affected by disability.

Respite care can be a great time for the kids, but the real beneficiaries are the parents. You won't be surprised, given all of Chapter 2, to hear that I believe the parents of preteens with special needs deserve the bulk of our attention and support. These are the daily advocates for the children who struggle, and these parents often experience rejection, judgment, loss, and loneliness because of their child's needs or behavior. Parenting is hard enough, but parenting a child with a disability is like swimming upstream, carrying a child, wearing a backpack and waterlogged boots. In the rain. We can help!

Serving parents affected by disability

Parents of kids with disabilities have an utterly different life and parenting experience than parents of kids without a diagnosis. Most parents in general live with feelings of guilt or anxiety regarding their kids' health, happiness, and performance, I would say. Add repeated instances of rejection, phone calls from school with bad news, and the child's own struggles, and we can understand why parents of kids with special needs are at their limit.

It wrings my heart to admit that the church has often contributed to the rejection that these families feel. Keep in mind that when working with a family affected by disability, there are unknown precursors under the surface. They likely won't share their full family and church context with us beforehand. In her blog at *The Inclusive Church* on February 14, 2014, Amy Fenton Lee posted:

> By the time a family approaches you to talk about their child's needs, countless conversations and mental hurdles have already passed at that point. It's like entering a conversation halfway through. See that conversation through the parents' context as much as possible. Consider all the hurt, expectations and fear that are wrapped up in their words.

Again, even if we do not know exactly how we are going to accommodate a particular child, our message to the parents is that we will figure it out together. We cannot step in with answers on our own as staff people—we can't take over from the parents. But we can work together with them to find a place of belonging that works. The solution may not be ideal, but there always is one.

One encouragement that we can offer to parents affected by disability is that their care and advocacy for their child is a beautiful thing. Some scholars have found that helping parents to see that their kids are their calling and loving them is doing God's work has helped to mitigate some of the stress of parenting. While I love the concept of parenting as a calling, it's essential that we not confuse that belief with the idea that God caused the disability or gives disability to any family for any reason. As I tell my kids in worship all the time, God only gives us good things. It is possible to learn from trials and even to rejoice in them, but God does not ordain pain or stress in our lives.

It is worth noting that the parents of kids with disabilities are more stressed by the behaviors that stem from the disability than by the disability itself. This leads me to blame our cultural expectations, in the church and elsewhere, that say if a child acts contrary to social norms the parents must have screwed up along the way. If we could release parents from the judgment and pressure that come from the other members of the church body about their kids' behavior, we would be a lot closer to ministering to the deep, spiritual needs these parents have for support, acceptance, and growth.

Final thoughts

In preparation for writing this chapter, I interviewed Dr. Steve Grcevich, president of Key Ministry, and he gave me some advice that I will leave you with now. First, every church needs to define their own "win" scenario. For some, a win could consist of simply making a meaningful connection between church staff and the family in need of support. Another possible win could be just keeping the kids safe and loved while their parents worship. Every church is different—start by considering your own church's goals and strengths, and decide what success looks like before a family even walks through the door.

Second, have no regard for the size of your church. Anyone can put out a welcome mat for every kind of family that might come. It's so much more about having a willing heart than any special knowledge or a dedicated sensory room or expert volunteers. Inclusive ministry is not a program; it is more like an attitude. People know when they are wanted, so show every preteen and every parent that you want them to meet God and receive God's love in your church. Make a space for every preteen, one at a time.

CHAPTER 6

IMPLEMENT

> When the Pharisees heard that Jesus had left the
> Sadducees speechless, they met together. One of
> them, a legal expert, tested him. "Teacher, what is the
> greatest commandment in the Law?"
>
> He replied, *"You must love the Lord your God with all
> your heart, with all your being,* and with all your mind.
> This is the first and greatest commandment. And the
> second is like it: *You must love your neighbor as you
> love yourself.* All the Law and the Prophets depend on
> these two commands." *(Matthew 22:34-40)*

It's so easy to be a modern-day Pharisee, y'all. I do it all the time. I mean, seriously, when confronted with a problem, the Pharisees called a meeting? Because, of course they did—meetings are our go-to.

It doesn't take a committee to figure out how to implement the ministry philosophy of this book: we must put relationships first. Love God and love others. The previous chapters shared theories of putting parents first, including every single kid, and giving preteens opportunities to discern their callings. The following models are just a few practical ideas for how to do this.

There's more than one way to do it . . .

. . . but not all the ways will work. I fully anticipate that anyone who reads through these practices who have worked for me will tweak them to fit their own style and church setting, and I love that. We all tend to evolve our personal strategy for ministry to kids, and figuring out your personal style is part of becoming a professional. There is definitely more than one way to structure your ministry in order to love preteens and empower their parents! Please make all my ideas your own—implement them in the way that works for you. While there are many ways to do preteen ministry well, there are also a few pitfalls that will not work at all. Here are some common pitfalls to avoid.

Don't let tradition dictate the future

The first is to rely on tradition, which sounds very much like what got the Pharisees in so much trouble. Chances are that wherever you are serving, you have inherited some events and expectations from the person who preceded you or the families you serve. And it is almost a certainty that the other leaders who help to plan and implement your ministry have brought their own experiences and expectations to the table.

But let's all agree—we do not make decisions based upon what has always been done. When people complain about changes you make and their first rationale is, "That's the way we've always done it," realize that they are not responding to your intentions or the quality of your ideas. They are struggling with change.

How do we respond when someone complains that a new initiative takes the place of a beloved experience? First, we choose to be grateful that God has revealed to us someone with enough passion to react that strongly at all. Then, we pounce and recruit that person to join our preteen ministry team to help craft the overall direction of the ministry. We make that person an insider, let them hear our exciting ideas for next-level discipleship, and give them a stake in the decisions that are made. We pull those traditionalists closer and let them flex their own design muscles and start to get interested in the changes we're making. We turn their fear into advocacy.

Most of all, we do not capitulate and start pulling all-nighters to produce an event or continue a program that a few people piped up about. As ministry workers, we must be prudent about the way we spend our time. The idea that all ministers lack work/life boundaries and that we should work sixty hours a week to earn our part-time salaries is a lie, and we need to stop living it. We need to recognize that it is immoral to break ourselves just to avoid a few complaints.

I feel like I have really superb advice in this area because I have tried all the wrong ways to handle it myself and found that they don't work. One year into my role as Director of Children's Ministries at a large church, I realized something about myself: I detest event planning. The previous director had been awesome at events. She had provided some truly meaningful memories and connections for people through the Easter festival and the family nights and the overnight retreats. As I tried to re-create the same schedule of events she had maintained, I felt like my whole year was spent scanning craft websites and ordering catering. So, I started to purge the schedule. Without telling anyone.

My staff suggested that people might really be upset, but I insisted that throwing a huge birthday bash for Jesus was not really going to help us make disciples and that I wanted to use that budget line for something more lasting. As Christmas drew near, families began to ask when Jesus' birthday party would be, and I would excitedly explain that we were funneling those resources into a different ministry area this year. To my utter surprise, those conversations often ended in tears and shocked looks. One parent looked me straight in the eye and said since I had been hired, I had taken Jesus out of Christmas for their family. In my shame, I just wanted to dig in deeper. I just knew I was right! But I had stolen something valuable from those families who were counting on it, and I had made that maverick decision all on my own. Don't do what I did.

Instead, it really helps if you clue your supervisor and pastor in before you switch up a whole ministry schedule on the people. And it's even better if you can pull together a group of trusted parents and advisers to get their ideas and blessing before that. Presenting an idea on behalf of a group of reputable leaders carries much more weight than simply throwing out your own ideas for approval. And chances are the final product will be much higher quality after you run it through this focus group first.

"Program" is a dirty word

If the first no-no is to allow tradition to shape your ministry, the second is to develop programs instead of models. A program is an end unto itself. It is a set of activities and curriculum that will keep the leaders and the kids busy and possibly provide a super fun time, but that ultimately distracts from our real focus: people. A model is a plan that puts relationships first. It is a structure that relies on adults who will demonstrate faith to kids, and it puts the kids first. Models are often not sexy at all. They rarely require eye-popping graphics and have nothing to do with your color scheme.

In *Almost Christian,* Kenda Creasy Dean writes that we tend to rely on programs because we're scared to get too personal with our faith. But to preteens, programs simply present God as an impersonal construct, a dry and distant deity rather than a loving and holy friend. The church's twentieth-century traditional model of Sunday school is based on the information-sharing models of elementary school, and it is not working. Faith is not information to be taught; it must be demonstrated.

I contend that programs are not just ineffective—they are dangerous. In a program mentality, it makes sense to prescribe a curriculum and a classroom to achieve spiritual development or to ask kids to raise their hands as you pray a sinner's prayer and then announce in worship the next week how many souls you saved. In programs, kids are just numbers. If your primary concern on Sunday mornings is whether or not you procured all the props and coloring sheets that your curriculum calls for, you are producing a program. If you find yourself regularly working late into the night to finalize all the details necessary to be ready for Sunday, you are producing a program. If your ministry times feel chaotic and you can't remember a single meaningful conversation you had with a preteen or parent at the end of the day, you are producing a program.

No more programs! Switch to a model that meets the needs of the individual kids in your ministry. Check out a few of my favorites.

Milestones

Or rites of passage or stepping stones or paths of discipleship or faith markers or whatever you and your community would like to call them. I love the idea of milestones the same way I love chocolate—with passion and dedication. Talking about this idea of structuring all family discipleship around significant faith moments in a kid's life is one of my favorite things.

Milestones are significant, developmentally-appropriate events in a person's life where we stop to rejoice in their growth and plan for the next stage of their spiritual journey. During any visit to a pediatrician, families receive a list of developmental milestones to expect for their child's age. I believe the church can offer spiritual milestones for each stage as well. Celebrating a milestone involves three acts: recognizing the child, equipping the parents, and calling for the support of the whole congregation. For each milestone, I generally give the child or family a tangible gift that will represent that moment for them forever.

One of the great benefits of celebrating a milestone with preteens is that it presents a totally nonthreatening opportunity to pull parents into conversation through the parent meeting. It's hard to get parents of this age group to come in the door and open up to you about their struggles and needs. However, coming together to celebrate achievement is in our DNA, and parents do this all the time for their kids. Parents who have never said two words to me before will often attend a milestone event for their child and then participate in the parent session willingly. That parent meeting is our opportunity to speak encouragement and conviction into the lives of our families. The value of celebrating a milestone for the preteen is real, but the investment it allows you to make in the whole family is unquantifiable.

You can almost choose anything as your church's preteen milestone(s). Some churches overachieve by celebrating a milestone for every age group, every year. I tend to want a milestone celebration for every two to three years in the life of a child, and every two to four years in the lives of youth. I will point out several options here and outline the way I would approach them, but you should truly make this your own.

Faith and sexuality milestone

As I belabored already in this book, I believe that the preteen years are by far the most appropriate time to introduce a faith and sexuality ministry in your church. If you are already pouring a lot of time and energy into such a ministry, why not weave it into your milestones strategy? It already contains the parent component where you bring parents together to equip them to participate in conversations about sexuality at home. It is already appropriate only for a certain age and developmental stage. All that remains is to create a congregational component and identify a tangible symbol for kids to take home.

Often during our faith and sexuality retreats, we will have the kids make some creation with their hands, using crafting wire or clay. By participating in a creative act, they understand in a new way that they are examples of God's own creativity. God created us with the ability to continue creating beautiful things. That creation craft can be a visual reminder of the milestone that recognized how wonderfully made they are. Other possible tangible symbols for this milestone could be a framed prayer of blessing over their bodies, a letter that parents are asked to write to them and give on the first or final day of the retreat, or a framed photo of the whole group that participates in the retreat.

For this kind of event, a simple announcement to the congregation to be in prayer for the preteens and their families as they journey to understand their identities as God's children is appropriate. You could also call the kids who will participate to the front of the church the Sunday before the retreat begins to pray over them, bless them, and ask God to instill in them a love for God, for self, and for others.

Small Groups

We could probably argue this next point for all of time to come, but I think sixth grade is a great year to begin emphasizing the importance of small-group discipleship. Many youth groups and middle schools start with sixth grade, which means that these preteens are thrust into contact with older and more experienced kids even though they likely are not ready for the decisions and opportunities that come with those older groups. In larger churches that can sustain a whole class of sixth-graders, I advocate for a separate path for this group. They can certainly be considered a part of youth group, but they are in a completely different stage than everyone else, and they should be allowed to circle their wagons and focus on their own small group before branching into the rest of youth group in seventh grade. In smaller churches, incorporate sixth-graders into the rest of the youth group very intentionally by introducing them to the group in an overtly protective manner, and inviting the older kids to shepherd these newest members of the group.

A small-group milestone allows church leaders to pull parents aside at the beginning of a school year, ostensibly to talk about what their kids will experience in this safe, cocooned group at church, but with the hidden motive of checking in with parents about how they are truly doing and learning what supports they need. Parents of sixth-graders can often feel at a loss for how to parent through this tricky stage, and it's no wonder. There is no perfect prescription for what freedoms, friendships, and conversations to allow for a sixth-grader. Every parent has to make it up on the go for each individual preteen, and that can be a real confidence buster. During the parent component of this milestone celebration, spend eighty percent of your time inviting parents to ask questions and share experiences with one another.

While there are some milestones that merit face time with the whole congregation, this one is personal and internal. During this time, the focus is on keeping these kids safe from the influences that both entice and terrify them and on equipping their parents to disciple them through serious ups and downs, so it makes sense to keep the celebration more private. By telling families that your sixth-grade milestone is an emphasis on small groups, you redefine the social anxieties of this stage in a positive way and communicate to parents that you will help to guide their kids through appropriate interactions.

Freedoms

One very simple way to recognize the preteen years as a milestone is to offer freedoms that only apply to this age group. For example, designate fourth- through sixth-graders to serve as acolytes during worship. For those of you whose worship services are more casual, an acolyte can be anyone who simply lights the candles in worship. Personally, I think I could find a way to incorporate candles into even the most laid-back worship services! And giving preteens the responsibility for lighting and/or extinguishing those candles during worship not only makes that task a privilege, it also keeps them engaged in worship. Again, having a role to play creates a sense of belonging, and in these preteen years we need to cultivate that kind of affinity for worship in any way we can.

Another freedom I like to allow beginning in fourth grade is self-dismissal. Up until this age, kids can only be released directly to their parents after ministry time for security purposes. After obtaining one-time permission from parents, I like to allow their kids in fourth grade on up to self-dismiss at the appointed end of the ministry time and trust them to make their way to their parents. The kids think that this is a huge favor we are doing them, but let's be honest, it is really a gift to their folks.

These milestone suggestions are merely starter ideas—take them for what they are and make them your own! The next preteen ministry model I will present here could certainly be incorporated into a milestone ministry, but it can also stand alone as a distinct model. It is one of the preteen ministries I am most excited about because it ties together everything I've said about calling and belonging in previous chapters. You already know this one! Let's say it together . . .

Apprenticeship

Little excites me more in my church ministry than working with preteens in apprenticeship. This model allows kids to opt in to the areas of service that exercise their preferred intelligence, from musical to hands-on to physical skills. While an apprenticeship ministry is more manageable in small or medium-sized churches, the right leadership team can implement this model in large churches as well.

102

Apprenticeship is a yearlong commitment by a preteen to serve in one area of the church under the guidance of an unrelated adult mentor from the congregation and with the support of the parents. In my church, we offer apprenticeship during fourth and fifth grade. During the summer, I meet individually with the families of incoming fourth-graders to complete a self-discovery exercise and talk about the areas of the church the preteen is interested in learning more about. The parents, the preteen, and I all contribute our thoughts about the preteen's gifts and interests. Together, we identify the area in which the preteen would like to serve, as well as several adults who could serve as the preteen's mentor in that area.

We start by asking the preteen which people or ministries they have noticed on their own and want to know more about. If they need prompting, I list several areas of service, such as nursery, preschool ministry, A/V team, hospitality, worship leadership (reading Scripture, leading liturgy, helping with announcements), worship coordination (attendance, taking offering, setting up Communion), music, and so forth.

Once we identify an apprenticeship area, we discuss the parameters that must be followed to keep the preteen safe and on the right track. For example, if a preteen wants to serve in children's ministry, that means he or she will not experience a worship service during that hour. The preteen and parents must agree to make worship attendance a higher priority than serving in apprenticeship. If they can only make it to one hour of the church morning, that hour should be spent in the sanctuary, not in the nursery.

We also talk about which freedoms and tasks the preteen is expected to fulfill and which things to avoid. There may be certain areas of the church that are off-limits or certain times of the morning when the preteen should not be in the sound booth or should give the mentor space. We discuss how to work with a mentor closely without violating any safety standards, such as meeting together only in public places and having a parent or second adult present.

Then we work together to identify an adult who is already active in the preteen's area of interest and could serve as a mentor for the year. As the staff person, I make the initial ask, and once I get the green light, I have the preteen approach this adult. By asking first, you avoid the possibility that a preteen could be turned down for this honor.

However you decide to define the mentor relationship, it needs to be communicated clearly to all parties. I ask that mentors serve alongside their apprentice at least once a month during church times, and that they meet outside church with their apprentice at least once a semester to get to know one another and debrief their serving experiences. There are a couple of questionnaires in the appendix that I use to help mentors, parents, and preteens set goals for the year and evaluate how well they have achieved them. Either at the beginning of the year or the end, we all get together for a meal to celebrate the preteen's apprenticeship and honor the preteen for her or his ministry.

The benefits of an apprenticeship abound. These experiences play directly into the calling stories for these kids. Not every person is called to a career in the church, but I do believe every person is called to serve in the church in some capacity. Apprenticeship raises up lifelong church leaders. This ministry also gives every preteen an identity and a job to do while at church. In my small community, we do not have a designated Sunday school hour on Sunday mornings. The only specific children's ministries take place during the worship services and end at third grade. Apprenticeship allows a preteen to be present all morning long and still always have something to do.

Apprenticeship also fulfills my one-person-at-a-time mantra by customizing the preteen's ministry time around that preteen's own needs and skills. Every preteen can apprentice in the church because the ministry is built on relationships, not on conformity or the needs of a group. There is no limit to the areas of the church where preteens can be included in some way, and once apprenticeship is an accepted model for your church, you'll have second- and third-graders submitting their preferred service areas to you years in advance.

Last and also least, if finding volunteers for Sunday morning is a struggle for you, I can't think of a better way to recruit more adults to serve than by saying, "A child has personally requested you as a mentor in our sound booth/kitchen/greeting team on Sunday mornings. Would you commit to serving with him?" You try to say no to that.

Bible Study

One of my favorite things to do in the whole wide world is to sit down with a small group of preteens and get their take on the Bible. All of their heartfelt, well-intentioned heresy comes out, and we bombard one another with questions until everyone feels they've discovered the insides and outsides of that Bible passage. Kids that grow up in the church spend every week from nursery until now learning the little-kid versions of Bible stories. For the preschool crowd, Jonah and the whale is a super fantastic story about a big fish, and Moses' parting the Red Sea provides a fun, sensory experience. This is all good and well—it is what it should be.

Somewhere between fourth and sixth grade, however, kids develop the ability to question and go deeper. They are ready to exercise those abstract-thinking muscles at the same time that they need to be treated differently than the younger age groups they've emerged from. The preteen years are the time to introduce kids to the practice of biblical exegesis and discussion. It is time to start instilling in them a love for basic spiritual practices like prayer, Bible study, serving, and deep friendships. And there's no better context for all these things than a small gathering of peers. My recipe for a transformative Bible study experience for preteens includes icebreakers, Bible reading, journaling, exploring the passage, lots of questions, and of course, snacks.

Icebreakers

I'm not going to belabor this point—we can likely all agree that starting a deep discussion with friendly get-to-know-you activities can be helpful. There is a list of icebreaker ideas at the end of this book to get you started. This activity should only take five to seven minutes.

Bible reading

When choosing a section of the Bible to study with preteens, give them as much power as possible. If you're familiar at all with Scripture, you'll know that there are a couple of passages you probably don't want to get into with preteens just yet. I'm looking at you, Song of Solomon. And Leviticus. Save all that stuff for the high school ministry.

If we give our kids the option to choose what they study, they'll be way more into it. I like to choose an array of different options, provide brief descriptions of them, and then see what the kids decide. Here is an example of a list I might give to my preteen groups:

- **Genesis**—the story of Creation, the Fall, Noah's ark, Abraham and his sons, Joseph and his brothers. This book contains lots of famous children's stories that take on a whole new meaning when you start to ask questions about them.

- **Ecclesiastes**—a book that not many people discover as preteens, but one that reads a lot like a personal journal. This is a set of poems about life, wisdom, and attitudes—preteens can identify with at least two of those three things.

- **Jonah**—it's about more than just a large fish! Find out the real beginning and real ending of the story of Jonah, and put yourself in the sandals of someone who is really a lot like we are and who faced some mighty scary stuff whether he obeyed God or not.

- **Luke (or any of the Gospels, really)**—the story of Jesus' life from start to finish. You can't go wrong studying Jesus.

- **Acts**—talk about what happened after Jesus went back to heaven, learn about the church's first birthday, and follow the greatest missionary story of all time through the life of Paul. This is one of the most exciting and sometimes funniest books of the Bible.

- **Philippians**—this book is really a letter that Paul sent to a group of Christians, and it covers a broad range of topics. The inspirational tone and beautiful language are full of deep meaning, and the whole book is full of verses the kids will recognize but have perhaps never thought much about before.

Clearly, some of these books are bigger than others. You can't simply choose Genesis or Luke and then read through the book verse by verse each week—some books require a bit more picking and choosing from the leader. Give the group just one chapter or a few verses to study each time they meet, and assign them the homework of reading the next week's passage before they come.

When you meet together and after you've settled in with an icebreaker, read that week's passage out loud together. This is probably stating the obvious, but when you read Scripture to your preteens, imbue it with all the feeling and fervor you can muster. Make conversations pop, and express surprise or outrage or intrigue or joy with your voice. Demonstrate how real to life Scripture is by reading it as if it was a thriller based on a true story. Which it is.

In the appendix, I provide a sample Bible study outline, which just offers methods preteens can use to explore the passage. Check it out!

Journaling

I don't know how long those composition notebooks have been around, but they cost about fifty cents each and make perfect journals. Grab one for each preteen in your group and use them as much as possible. Give your preteens the freedom to write or illustrate their thoughts, whichever works better for them. I'll often use journaling as a way to let the biblical passage we just read seep into their souls a bit before we dive into discussion, but sometimes we journal at the very end after we've already discussed the passage up one way and down the other.

Journaling is a truly inexhaustible resource. If you find you have ten more minutes to fill before the service ends, pull the journals out again! Kids should never be forced to share what they've logged in their journals, and if your Bible study takes place at the church, please find a safe place to store the journals where others can't waltz in and invade one another's privacy throughout the week.

Questions

There is no such thing as too many questions. The truth is, most of us probably don't have very many answers, so we should just spend as much time unpacking the questions as possible. The point is not to find answers but to teach kids how to reflect and meditate on God's words. Write down every single question that the kids ask, either by having them record them in their journals or by putting them on a markerboard for everyone to see.

But the kids shouldn't be the only ones bringing questions to the table. The small-group leaders have to read these passages in advance and come prepared with their own reflection questions as well. Encourage the kids to offer up their ideas in answer to questions, but try not to provide any answers yourself. (The exception to this rule is when kids veer off into heretical territory. I cherish the memory of once leading a discussion with fifth-grade boys when they reached consensus that Jesus must not have been fully human as well as fully divine. I did step in at that point.)

Prove to them that they can ask you anything that is on their minds, and you'll listen. You may not satisfy their curiosity, but you will encourage it.

Snacks

Don't judge—eating with loved ones is a sacred act, right? You try spending ninety minutes with preteens studying the Bible and entering into real conversation without some edible reinforcement and see how far you get. Their bodies are growing and changing constantly—it's no wonder they are constantly hungry. I believe healthy(ish) snacks are a key component to helping kids feel comfortable and open up. Break out the bagels with cream cheese, Greek yogurt with honey, fruit, plain popcorn, veggie tray, hummus dip, cheese sticks, dried fruit, or chips with salsa and guacamole. We can't get too high on the idea of spiritual transformation and deep friendships with preteens without accounting for their hollow legs.

Final thoughts

That's it! Those are some of my best ideas. They're all yours now. The first five chapters of this book are theoretical. They are my personal preteen ministry philosophy. This last chapter is merely practical, a list of ideas that have worked for me and that, with personalization, may work for you too. For that reason, there isn't a long list of sources to reference, since my research for these ideas emerged solely from my personal experience in ministry.

If God has called you to ministry with preteens, then dive in, friend. There's really no other age group that presents such a perfect window of ability and teachability as these fourth- through sixth-graders. Stick with them for a couple of years, and pretty soon you will be writing your own six secrets. I can't wait to read them!

APPENDICES

Appendix A: Great Icebreakers for Preteens

Google really has the answer for all the icebreakers you could ever need, but this list can serve as a quick, easy, and safe set of icebreaker questions that are appropriate for any group of preteens in the church.

Discussion Questions

1. What three words would you use to describe yourself?

2. If you gave life advice to a kindergartner, what would you say?

3. If you could only keep one or two of your current possessions for the rest of your life, what would they be?

4. What do you think is the perfect job?

5. What is the longest word you know?

6. If a genie offered you three wishes, what would you wish?

7. Which is better, birthdays or Christmas? Why?

8. If you could be invisible for a day, what would you do?

9. Would you rather be a genius or a movie star? Why?

10. Describe the best vacation you can imagine.

11. If you could be any animal, which one would you choose?

12. Tell us about something you've made before—food, a work of art, a tool, and so forth.

13. What is your favorite ice cream flavor?

14. What is your favorite book?

15. Which famous person would you like to meet?

16. Tell us your favorite joke.

17. What is something about you that nobody else here knows?

18. What is your favorite time of day—morning, afternoon, or evening—and why?

19. If you could be one age forever, which age would you choose?

20. If you could change your name, would you? What name would you choose?

21. If you could get only one item for your birthday or Christmas, what would you want?

22. Picture your bedroom. Tell us about the first small object you think of that is in your room.

23. How would you like to make the world a better place?

24. What is the weirdest thing you've ever eaten?

25. What is the most beautiful thing in the world?

26. What is the latest you have stayed up before bed?

27. Name one fictional character that you wish were real.

28. Tell us about a time when God answered a prayer.

29. Tell us a Bible verse or story from memory.

30. What is your earliest memory from your childhood?

31. What is your favorite sport to watch? to play?

32. Would you rather be invisible or able to read people's minds?

33. What are two things you do really well?

34. Name one song that you know all the lyrics to by heart.

35. What is your biggest fear?

36. Which are better pets, dogs or cats?

37. If you could live one day over again from your life, which day would you pick?

38. Which household chore do you dislike the most?

39. If you could only listen to one song for the rest of your life, what would it be?

40. What is the best Halloween costume you've worn?

41. What toppings do you like on your pizza?

42. Which drink do you get when you're at a soda machine?

43. If you discovered a new island, what would you name it?

44. If you had to be trapped in a TV show for a month, which show would you choose?

45. How long does it take you to get ready for school in the morning?

46. If you could go back in time and change history, what would you change?

47. Tell us about a time when you took a huge leap of faith.

48. Who is your role model?

49. What is your favorite smell?

50. Tell us about one thing you didn't understand when you were little, but now you get it.

Icebreaker Activities

1. **Mix & Meet M&M's**—Have each kid grab a small handful of M&M's. Instruct them not to eat any yet. Assign a category to each candy color, such as: Blue = family, Green = school, Yellow = friends, Red = hobbies, Brown = music/movies. Invite the students to share something about themselves within the appropriate category for each M&M they eat.

2. **Three Things in Common**—Divide the kids into groups of three or four. Each group must find three things they have in common with each other—the weirder, the better. After five minutes, each

group announces the things they have in common. Then everyone votes on which group found the weirdest things in common.

3. **Sit Down If**—Everyone stands in a circle while the leader asks a range of silly questions. Kids must sit down anytime their answer to the question is yes. Questions can be as random as you like, such as, "Did you eat cheese today?" or "Are your shoes untied?" or "Have you ever ridden a camel?" The last person standing gets to ask questions for the next round.

4. **Toilet Paper Pass**—Hold on to the tail of the toilet paper roll and throw the rest of the roll to someone across from you in the circle. The person who catches the roll must say one thing about himself or herself. Then, that person holds on to the tail and throws the roll to someone else. If the toilet paper tail breaks, the person who threw it must share an extra personal fact.

5. **Me Shirts**—Ask each preteen to bring from home a T-shirt that they don't mind painting. (Have a couple of extras on hand for anyone who needs one.) Provide fabric markers or puffy paint and ask the kids to design a shirt that is all about themselves. If a shirt is already covered in screen printing, turn it inside out to decorate. Then have them model their shirts for one another and explain what they created.

Appendix B: Sample Bible Study Outline

You don't need to purchase a curriculum with all the bells and whistles in order to provide a meaningful Bible study time with preteens. This outline can incorporate just about any passage. Pick and choose the sections each time—there is way too much here for any one session.

Read the Scripture Aloud

- The adult reads it with feeling or one preteen reads to the group or the group reads in unison.

Seek & Find

Ask the group to identify what they believe are the most important words in the passage. Invite them to explain why they chose each word. Write the meaningful words on a board or on sticky notes.

Where Is God?

See if you can identify where God is at work in the passage you read together. Is Jesus in the passage? Is God speaking to someone? How does this section lead up to Jesus' death and resurrection?

Lectio Divina or Meditation

Ask the group to get super quiet. Let them sit comfortably, either lounging on couches or lying on the floor. Consider playing soft music in the background. Tell them you will read the passage to them several times, and they should listen in a different way each time.

- First, just listen to each individual word and take them all in.
- Second, listen for only one or two words that stand out to them.
- Third, listen for what God is saying to them through those words.

Modern-day Version

As a group, work together to rewrite the passage in your own language. If your passage was a story, give the characters modern-day names, occupations, and descriptions. If your passage was not a story, look at several different biblical translations to find the right meaning, and paraphrase it. Share with each other examples of how the passage applies to your everyday life.

Outline

Make a bulleted list of the main points. Then, have one person retell the story or the passage in her own words, using only the outline.

Ask Questions

Make a long list of all the questions you could ask about the passage. Don't worry about answering them, but record them on a markerboard or on note cards.

Exegesis

Grab an iPad or a computer for this one. Download a Bible app that provides commentary and/or the original Greek or Hebrew definitions. Some good apps to start with are Logos or YouVersion Bible, both of which are free. If you are strapped for technology, a good hard copy of a concordance and several different versions of the Bible will do.

Explore the passage you are reading down to its most basic parts. Let the kids take the lead on this—the adults in the room do not need to be biblical scholars and can let the kids do most of the investigating on their own. Have the kids present their findings.

Prayer

This may be the most important part of any Bible study! Make sure to save time, every time, to talk to God about what you have explored together. You can pray in several ways: let the kids journal their prayers privately; pass out blank papers and lots of colorful markers, and have them pray in color by drawing or illustrating their responses to the Scripture; let each person pray out loud; pray over the group as the leader; collaborate to write out a prayer on a markerboard or on mural paper.

Blessing

At the end of any study time, speak a blessing over each individual child in the group. You can either bless each preteen personally or you can have them bless one another.

To give a blessing, use a new tube of lip balm to make the sign of the cross on the back of a kid's hand while saying your version of "You are a blessing. Now go and bless others." Let the kids sit in a circle and bless one another, making the sign of the cross and then passing the lip balm on to the next person.

Appendix C: Apprenticeship Forms

I ask the apprentice, the parent(s), and the mentor to complete a form, and then we refer to it throughout the year together.

Apprentice Form

My name:	
Name(s) of parent(s):	
My mentor's name:	
My three goals for this apprenticeship:	1. 2. 3.
Three things I think I do really well:	1. 2. 3.
Some of the coolest adult jobs I know of are:	1. 2. 3.
Our meeting plan: I will meet with my mentor _____ times each week / month / semester / year.	
Serving together: I will serve with my mentor _____ times each week / month / semester / year.	

Mentor Form

Mentor Name:	
Apprentice Name:	
My three goals for this apprenticeship:	1. 2. 3.
Three gifts I see in my apprentice:	1. 2. 3.
Three ways I hope to grow as a mentor:	1. 2. 3.
Our meeting plan: We will meet _____ times each week / month / semester / year.	
Serving together: I will serve with my apprentice _____ times each week / month / semester / year.	

Parent Form

Parent(s) Name(s):	
Apprentice Name:	
My three goals for this apprenticeship:	1. 2. 3.
Three gifts I see in my child:	1. 2. 3.
Three lifelong endeavors I could see my child doing are:	1. 2. 3.
Our meeting plan: My child and his/her mentor will meet _____ times each week / month / semester / year.	
My commitment: I will transport and communicate so my child can serve with his/her mentor _____ times each week / month / semester / year.	

REFERENCES

Chapter 1

Berger, Kathleen Stassen. *The Developing Person Through the Life Span.* 5th ed. New York: Worth Publishers, 2001.

Berk, Laura E. *Child Development.* 7th ed. Boston: Pearson Education, Inc., 2006.

Carter, Betty and McGoldrick, Monica. *The Expanded Family Life Cycle: Individual, Family, and Social Perspectives.* 3rd ed. New York: Pearson Education, 2005.

Crouter, Ann C. and Booth, Alan. *Romance and Sex in Adolescence and Emerging Adulthood: Risks and Opportunities.* New York: Routledge, 2016.

Hamner, Tommie J. and Turner, Pauline H. *Parenting in Contemporary Society.* 4th ed. Boston: Allyn & Bacon, 2001.

Chapter 2

American Psychological Association. "Ethnic and Racial Minorities & Socioeconomic Status." Accessed May 22, 2017. *www.apa.org/pi/ses/resources/publications/minorities.aspx*

Berk, Laura E. *Child Development.*

Boyatzis, Chris J. "Spiritual Development During Childhood and Adolescence," in *The Oxford Handbook of Psychology and Spirituality,* 151–164. New York: Oxford University Press, 2014.

Carter, Betty and McGoldrick, Monica. *The Expanded Family Life Cycle: Individual, Family and Social Perspectives.*

Creasy Dean, Kenda. *Almost Christian: What the Faith of Our Teenagers Is Telling the American Church.* New York: Oxford University Press, 2010.

Joiner, Reggie and Ivy, Kristen. *It's Just a Phase—So Don't Miss It: Why Every Life Stage of a Kid Matters and at Least 13 Things Your Church Should Do About It.* Cumming, GA: Orange Books, 2015.

National Center for Children in Poverty. "Child Poverty." Accessed May 22, 2017. *nccp.org/topics/childpoverty.html*

National Science Foundation. "Table 1-1. Resident population of the United States, by age and sex: 2014." Accessed May 22, 2017. *https://www.nsf.gov/statistics/2017/nsf17310/static/data/tab1-1.pdf*

Mahoney, Annette and Krumrei, Elizabeth J. "Questions Left Unaddressed by Religious Familism: Is Spirituality Relevant to Nontraditional Families?" in *The Oxford Handbook of Psychology and Spirituality*, 165–181. New York: Oxford University Press, 2014.

Petts, Richard J. "Parental Religiosity and Youth Religiosity: Variations by Family Structure," in *Sociology of Religion,* Vol. 76, Issue 1 (2014): 95–120.

Pew Research Center. December 17, 2015. "Parenting in America." Accessed May 22, 2017. *http://www.pewsocialtrends.org/2015/12/17/1-the-american-family-today/*

Chapter 3

Buechner, Frederick. *Wishful Thinking: A Theological ABC.* New York: Harper & Row, 1973.

Cepeda, Esther J. "Jaime Casap: From Tough Childhood to Google's Global Education Evangelist." NBC News. Accessed May 22, 2017. *www.nbcnews.com/news/latino/jaime-casap-tough-childhood-google-s-global-education-evangelist-n627781*

Corsaro, William A., Molinari, Luisa, and Brown Rosier, Katherine. "Zena and Carlotta: Transition Narratives and Early Education in the United States and Italy," in *Human Development* Vol. 45, no. 5 (2002): 323–348.

Dik, Byran J., Duffy, Ryan D., and Eldridge, Brandy M. "Calling and Vocation in Career Counseling: Recommendations for Promoting Meaningful Work," in *Professional Psychology: Research and Practice,* Vol. 40, no. 6 (2009): 625–632.

Erikson, Erik. *Childhood and Society.* New York: Norton, 1963.

Huston, A.C. *Developmental Contexts in Middle Childhood: Bridges to Adolescence and Adulthood.* Cambridge, UK: Cambridge University Press, 2006.

Josephus. *Antiquities of the Jews* 5.10.4. Accessed May 22, 2017. *sacred-texts.com/jud/josephus/ant-5.htm*

Schuurman, Douglas J. *Vocation: Discerning Our Callings in Life.* Grand Rapids: Eerdmans, 2003.

Chapter 4

Abel, Gene G. and Harlow, Nora. *The Stop Child Molestation Book: What Ordinary People Can Do in Their Everyday Lives to Save Three Million Children.* Philadelphia: Xlibris, 2001.

Berger, Kathleen Stassen. *The Developing Person Through the Life Span.*

Berk, Laura E. *Child Development.*

Buying into Sexy: The Sexing Up of Tweens. New York: Films Media Group, 2005. 26 min.

Centers for Disease Control and Prevention. "About Behavioral Risk Factor Surveillance System ACE Data." Accessed May 22, 2017. *https://www.cdc.gov/violenceprevention/acestudy/ace_brfss.html*

Christian, Cindy W. "The Evaluation of Suspected Child Physical Abuse," in *Pediatrics* 135, no. 5 (2015): 1337–1354.

Influence Central. "Kids & Tech: The Evolution of Today's Digital Natives." Accessed May 22, 2017. *influence-central.com/kids-tech-the-evolution-of-todays-digital-natives/*

King, Cheryl A., Ewell Foster, Cynthia, and Rogalski, Kelly M. *Teen Suicide Risk: A Practitioner Guide to Screening, Assessment, and Management.* London: Guilford Press, 2013.

Magahern, Jimmy. "Small World." *Dallas Observer*. December 20, 2001. *http://www.dallasobserver.com/music/small-world-6394967*.

Mazzarella, Sharon R. "Advertising Targeting of Tweens." *Encyclopedia of Children, Adolescents, and the Media,* Vol 2. Thousand Oaks, CA: Sage, 2007.

Miyazaki, Anthony D., Stanaland, Andrea J.S., and Lwin, May O. "Self-Regulatory Safeguards and the Online Privacy of Preteen Children," in *The Journal of Advertising,* Vol. 38, no. 4 (Winter 2009): 79–91.

The Henry J. Kaiser Family Foundation. "Generation M2: Media in the Lives of 8- to 18-Year-Olds." Accessed May 22, 2017. *http://kff.org/other/report/generation-m2-media-in-the-lives-of-8-to-18-year-olds/*

Tough, Paul. *How Children Succeed: Grit, Curiosity, and the Hidden Power of Character.* Boston: Houghton Mifflin Harcourt, 2012.

Chapter 5

Carter, Betty and McGoldrick, Monica. *The Expanded Family Life Cycle: Individual, Family and Social Perspectives.*

Fenton Lee, Amy. "Understanding Parents (Parent-Church Conversations Part 1)." *The Inclusive Church* (blog). February 14, 2014. *theinclusivechurch.wordpress.com/2014/02/14/parent-church-conversations-part-1-understanding-parents/*

Nathaniel's Hope. *nathanielshope.org*

Peoples, Sandra. "What Special-Needs Families Really Want From the Churches We Attend." *Church4EveryChild* (blog). October 20, 2016. *http://www.keyministry.org/church4everychild/2016/10/20/what-special-needs-families-really-want-from-the-churches-we-attend*

Weyland, Chelsea, O'Laughlin, Liz, and Bennett, Patrick. "Dimensions of Religiousness That Influence Parenting," in *Psychology of Religion and Spirituality,* Vol. 5, no. 3 (August 2013): 182–191.

Azad, Gazi, Blacher, Jan, and Marcoulides, George A. "Mothers of children with developmental disabilities: Stress in early and middle childhood," in *Research in Developmental Disabilities,* Vol. 34, no. 10 (October 2013).

Chapter 6

Creasy Dean, Kenda. *Almost Christian: What the Faith of our Teenagers is Telling the American Church.*

SUGGESTED READING

Joiner, Reggie and Ivy, Kristen. *It's Just a Phase—So Don't Miss It: Why Every Life Stage of a Kid Matters and at Least 13 Things Your Church Should Do About It.* Cumming, GA: Orange Books, 2015.

Haynes, Brian. *Shift: What It Takes to Finally Reach Families Today.* Loveland, CO: Group Publishing Inc., 2009.

Bevins, Winfield. *Grow at Home: A Beginner's Guide to Family Discipleship.* Franklin, TN: Seedbed Publishing, 2016.

Eckmann Powell, Kara, Griffin, Brad M., and Crawford, Cheryl A. *Sticky Faith, Youth Worker Edition.* Grand Rapids: Zondervan, 2011.

Eckmann Powell, Kara, Mulder, Jake, and Griffin, Brad. *Growing Young: Six Essential Strategies to Help Young People Discover and Love Your Church.* Grand Rapids: Baker Books, 2016.

Brown, Terence. *The Before Project.* 2014. Short Film, 37:02. *thebeforeproject.org*

Guinness, Os. *The Call: Finding and Fulfilling the Central Purpose of Your Life.* Nashville: Thomas Nelson, Inc., 2003.

Steele, Jeremy. *SEX: A Christian Perspective on Our Bodies, Decisions and Relationships for 6th, 7th and 8th Grade Youth.* Nashville: Discipleship Ministries, 2014.

thinkb4u.com (A hokey but accurate site preteens can explore to learn about the power of online sharing.)

"Choose What Happens Next." YouTube video series by the National Center for Missing and Exploited Children. *youtube.com/watch?v=pGkaw44-QI4*

admongo.gov (A game-based website that teaches kids how to identify and interpret advertising.)

commonsensemedia.org (A one-stop shop for information about the influence of media on families, from movie reviews to research data.)

Miller, Anne Marie. *5 Things Every Parent Needs to Know About Their Kids and Sex.* Grand Rapids: Baker Books, 2016.

keyministry.org (A website dedicated to connecting local churches to families impacted by disabilty.)

Wetherbee, Katie and Philo, Jolene. *Every Child Welcome: A Ministry Handbook for Including Kids with Special Needs.* Grand Rapids: Kregel Publications, 2015.

irresistiblechurch.org (A website dedicated to helping churches become "authentic communities built on the hope of Christ that compels people affected by disability to fully belong.")

99balloons.org and *nathanielshope.org* (Websites providing excellent resources for starting or improving a respite care ministry.)

clcnetwork.org (Website that provides excellent information for inclusive school settings.)

Hadley, Leanne. *Blessed to be a Blessing.* Nashville: Discipleship Resources, 2016.

"Preteen Ministry: How to Nurture Preteens' Faith Development," in *Children's Ministry Magazine,* July 6, 2012. *childrensministry.com/articles/bridge-ministry-preteens/*

Refocus: A Ministry for Transition. "Types of Family Ministry." *refocusministry.org/resources-for-ministers/family-ministry/types-of-family-ministry/*

CPSIA information can be obtained
at www.ICGtesting.com
Printed in the USA
LVOW13s1205111217
559034LV00024B/42/P